letters home

From 9/11 to Operation Iraqi Freedom
A Military Mom Shares Her Family's Story
of Patriotism, Courage and Love

Sonia,
  Thank you for all you do
for our veterans.
        In Gratitude,
         Mary Ward
            6/15/2022

Mary Ward

First Edition
MareHaven Productions, Inc. • Durham, NC

"For the Strength of the Pack is the Wolf,
  and the strength of wolf is the pack"
      -Rudyard Kipling,
       The Jungle Book

Letters home
  From 9/11 to Operation Iraqi Freedom: A Military Mom Shares Her Family's
  Story of Patriotism, Courage and Love
  by Mary Ward

Published by:
MareHaven Productions, Inc.
PO Box 61562
Durham, NC 27715-1562
919-493-5039
Website: www.marehaven.com

Publisher's Cataloging-in-Publication (Provided by Quality Books, Inc.)
    Ward, Mary, 1960-
        Letters home : from 9/11 to Operation Iraqi Freedom :
    a military mom shares her family's story of patriotism,
    courage and love / Mary Ward. — 1st ed.
        p. cm.
        ISBN 0-9760172-0-2

    1. War on Terrorism, 2001- —Personal narratives,
    American. 2. Ward, Sean, 1983- —Correspondence.
    3. Soldiers—United States—Correspondence. 4. Ward, Mary,
    1960- —Correspondence. 5. Mothers of soldiers—United
    States—Correspondence.   I. Ward, Sean, 1983-
    II. Title.

HV6432.W374 2004   973.931'092'2
QBI04-200365
Printed in the United States of America

COVER:
Top left: The Great Seal of the United States. The seal is on the official Army
    writing paper.
Photograph: Taken of Sean minutes after he was reunited with us.
Medal: Reproduction of the Army Commendation Medal
Symbol placed as the letter "o" in home: Part of the Iraqi currency known as a dinar
Envelope: Envelope from a letter Sean sent home from Iraq
Letter: One of the first letters Sean wrote home from basic training
Cover design: Lacey Chylack

To my soulmate, Tom

for his belief in me long before I believed in myself, for his continuous encouragement and positive thoughts all of our years together, for making me laugh deeply and fully, for teaching me that self-actualization is more than a mere possibility but nearing reality each and every day.

C ONTENTS

INFANTRYMAN

IF YOU KNOW AN INFANTRYMAN and it's always a man, your father, your brother, your husband or maybe your son, you know a special kind of person. Special because the mission of the infantry is to close with and destroy the enemy. Close with means to close the gap between the enemy and the soldier. Destroy means to take this rifle and kill the enemy. The infantrymen will complete the mission or die trying. Infantry is a chosen occupation. An Infantryman is a special kind of person.

August, 2002

Mom + Dad,

It is day one of my official training. I have next to no time to write right now so I'm going to send you my address – please give it to everyone who will want it.

If there is a true emergency contact the Red Cross, they will notify me. More letters will follow soon:

Address

> *PFC Ward, Sean Thomas RN*
> *447 FCo 2/58 Infantry*
> *9375 Conway Dr*
> *Ft. Benning, GA 31905-5914*

Follow it to the letter please as is on my return address. I love you and write me a lot.

Its Extremely Hard but I like it.

> *PFC Ward*
> *XXOO*
> *P.S.*
> *Phones are earned you know?*
> *P.P.S. I miss you guys*

I.

Days of Innocence

Many moms are like me. We remember our pregnancies and talk about our children's births as if we were the only one on earth to have had the experience. We expect everyone around us to be enthralled by our birth stories, especially other women. We gather in small groups and suddenly a common thread connects us. We share our birth battles and all the excruciating, delightful details with one another. We can't help ourselves; childbirth is right up there as one of the greatest moments in our lives. At least it was for me until my son, Sean, an infantryman, came home from war.

August 8, 2003 - the details of that day, like childbirth, are etched in my heart and mind forever. It is the day Sean returned home from Operation Iraqi Freedom alive, intact and healthy. He was 20 years old. This was one of the most magnificent days of my life.

I have chosen to share our family story through the letters Sean wrote home from basic training to his last letter from Iraq as well as our thoughts and actions through the time of his homecoming. It is important to share the impact that terrorism and war have on families and soldiers. Our lives don't stop because of the terrorism and war, in fact, life races along relentlessly as did ours. Yet, for us, our hearts and minds came to a stand still until Sean was home safely.

Sean greeting Kate the day we brought her home from the hospital.
Sean learning at an early age the joy of playing in the mud.
A loose tooth and his dad's old Marine Corps. Hat – all is right in Sean's world.

After 3 miscarriages I finally had a healthy pregnancy, labor and birth with Sean. I went into labor the day before my due date just in time for a massive snowstorm. It was a rare Long Island blizzard. A state of emergency was issued which meant civilians were not permitted to be out on the road driving.

I was visiting my mom the day I went into labor and once it started to snow I stayed there because she didn't want me to be alone. My husband, Tom, was working in New York City at the time and it took him hours to get home. By the time he arrived at least 12 inches of new fallen snow blanketed the area. To get to the hospital we called for emergency transportation and before we knew it we had the police department, a county snow-plow and an ambulance simultaneously arrive at the house.

Due to the amount of snow and the size of my pregnancy I couldn't navigate the walk from the house to the ambulance. After a long, tiring day getting home in the storm, my brother, Kevin and Tom carved out a safe path in the snow for me. To assist the ambulance in a safe journey to the hospital the snow-plow cleared the roads and the police car provided a rear escort. It made for an interesting night as well as a good birth story!

Sean had been in the breech position for weeks but turned around a few days before I went into labor. He didn't quite make a complete turn and, therefore, wasn't in the proper birthing position. After something close to 15 hours Sean was finally born by emergency cesarean section. He was born on February 12, 1983 and was 10 lbs 2 oz., 23 inches long.

Tom and I decided that I would stay home with our children for as long as it was possible. With that in mind, we decided to have them close in age. I became pregnant with, my daughter, Kate when Sean was 10 months old. I loved being pregnant with her. However, early in the pregnancy I had a miscarriage scare so progression through each milestone was thrilling. Near the end of the pregnancy I would sometimes experience concern about being able to raise two kids. I had already had one so I knew very well the commitment it took. Once Kate was born I fell in love for the third time in my life. All of my concerns washed away.

We had another miscarriage when Kate was just a little over 2 years old. Shortly after that Tom and I decided not to have any more children. We had two beautiful children to raise and the loss caused by my miscarriages brought too much sadness; losing the last one on Christmas Day threw us over the edge. Neither one of us were willing to incur any more heartache. We took the positive approach and put our energy in to raising Sean and Kate.

Raising toddlers was the busiest time of my life; we had one car and a double stroller. I walked everywhere with the kids. Tom was working fulltime and going to college four nights a week. But somehow we managed to make it all work. When Tom was home he spent quality time with the kids. We devoted our weekends to the family.

Walking the kids into town was often an adventure. One time when my sister Jessica came to visit we walked the kids into town for a pizza lunch. It was a windy March day so we walked as fast as we could. On such walks Sean or Kate would typically drop a shoe or a pacifier along the way and we would have to backtrack. This day it was a clean walk. We made it there in record time. No sooner had I pushed the stroller through the door and parked it alongside the picture window when a woman drove her car through a four-foot high concrete planter and crashed into the store window. If we had been delayed for a few seconds we would have been standing right in the path of the oncoming car. The woman accidentally slammed on the gas instead of the brakes. It is estimated that the car was going 60 mph when she crashed.

The crash brought those who witnessed it to tears. The businessmen and women who were waiting in line for their lunch simply could not believe their eyes. As they walked past us they shared with me that they felt they had witnessed a miracle. I couldn't help but agree with them.

I remember standing at the counter, hearing the crash and looking back to see the car wedged into the window and my beautiful babies' inches from disaster. For a few seconds I felt suspended in time. Then I suddenly realized that I had to get them out of there quickly. Pieces of the ceiling had started to crumble and the glass window was shattered. It didn't occur to me until later that day how close I was to losing my children. I learned then that no matter how much I want to protect them there are some things in life that are out of my control.

Since that day I think of how many people the four of us have touched. Maybe that is why we lived. We were meant to be here to have a positive impact on others.

The years I spent raising my children taught me to deeply and selflessly love another human being. The sweet smell of my babies is etched into my memory forever. As they grew I remember how often I put their needs before my own without hesitation. It makes me smile to remember the many stages Sean and Kate went through that add up to a lifetime of loving and caring for them.

Tom and I were looking forward to providing a stable, loving home for our children. Tom worked fulltime and went to school at night to advance his career. It was often difficult for both of us. We knew the end result would be worth the struggle but that didn't make the time less draining. We had so little material goods in our early days together. Yet we always had a roof overhead, food on the table and clothes on our back. Through diligence, persistence and occasional support from our families we always managed to make ends meet.

"He's all boy!" Think how frequently mothers of sons have repeated that phrase. If we didn't say it, someone said it to us about our sons. It was a term often repeated in reference to Sean. More from others than from myself as I don't often think in clichés. Yet when I think of how to best describe Sean "all boy" enters my thoughts immediately.

Sean's favorite toys were GI Joes, a battery powered 4-wheel truck, and toy guns, which were very un-cool when he was a little boy. Before he had the toy guns he would play with sticks using them as guns. He called the sticks "smokers" and would make shooting sounds. Perhaps playing with guns is instinctual because he wasn't exposed to guns at home. I limited Sean's tel-

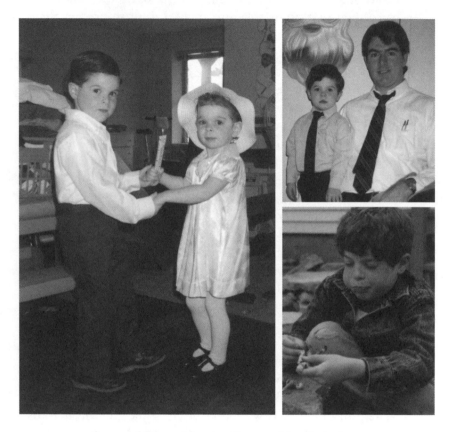

Sean and Kate celebrating Easter with a little dance.
Tom and Sean dressed for office work.
Sean playing with GI Joe was a familiar sight!

evision shows to children's programming on public television
and Tom didn't have guns in the house. When I watched him
play with sticks I feared for his safety. I took the sticks away but
nearly every time we went to the playground he found a new
one to use as a "smoker". I could see it was an argument I was
destined to lose so I bought him a plastic gun. In my world it
was safer than sticks. Although I will say the other mothers at
the park were not thrilled with my choice of toys for Sean.

I often had to explain to the mothers why I let him play with
toy guns. When I was two years old I was hit with a stick leaving me blind in the left eye. The injury happened because five
and six year old boys were playing Army with sticks and I was
caught in the crossfire. Sometimes the explanation was accepted and sometimes it wasn't. When it wasn't they would leave the
park with their kids upon our arrival.

The gun incidents wouldn't be the last time my peers dis-
agreed with how I raised my children. I developed a tolerance
for the moms who thought they knew better than I what was
best for my son. This would carry me through many years while
raising Sean and continues today.

Sean was also a territorial little guy. When we had other children play at the house he would walk around like he owned it.
When he was three and four years old he would take his shirt off
and strut around sticking his belly out. Of course the other kids
were never intimidated; they had no idea what he was doing. He
looked like a tribal chief staking out his piece of the land. As he
got older he would make signs with our family name on them
and nail them to trees in the front yard. When 9/11 occurred it
shouldn't have surprised me that he would be enraged by the violence perpetrated on his country, yet it did. It surprised me that
it affected him deeply enough to do something about it.

Sean's favorite childhood activity was playing with GI Joe's.
He was a constant source of noise and adventure. One
Christmas all of his gifts were variations of GI Joe toys. It was
his favorite Christmas. Sean played with GI Joe until he was
about 12 years old. He was content to play for hours by himself

and was happy to discover friends who were partial to GI Joe.

Camouflage clothing was the "in" style for boys when Sean was young. However, Tom would not permit Sean to wear this type of clothing because he didn't want a military influence on him. He didn't talk much about his Marine Corps experience for the same reason. Naturally, this made Sean even more interested in this part of his dad's life.

Sean has always been crazy about his father. From the time Sean crawled he anticipated his dad's arrival from work. After his bath he listened for his dad's footsteps coming down the hall. To Sean his dad had a distinctive sound to his walk. As soon as Tom stepped off the elevator Sean raced to the front door, sat down and waited in eager anticipation of his dad's arrival. As soon as Tom opened the door he squealed with delight. Sean was justly rewarded with a bear hug, a toss in the air and smooches all over his face.

When he was three years old, Sean insisted on dressing in work clothes like his dad. He wore a dress shirt and tie for months. He even had a toy phone that he used to call an imaginary friend and make business deals. Being like his dad was where it was at for him.

The day came when Sean was about five years old that he found Tom's Marine Corps sea bag packed with his old uniforms including many hats. Finding the hats thrilled Sean. He put one on and rarely took it off. Tom didn't have the heart to take it away. Sean told me recently that he remembers how happy he was when he found the Marine Corps hat. He said his dad was his first hero and finding the sea bag full of uniforms and hats confirmed for him that his dad was a real life action figure. He remembers thinking how cool it was that his dad was a real GI Joe!

The other things that made Sean "all boy" were his love of playing in the dirt including covering himself and his sister in mud; a fascination with fire trucks and fireman uniforms; a dislike of cleaning his room ... any room for that matter and the ability to show no emotion while being scolded or punished.

If I had really looked I would have seen this "all boy" child for what he was – an infantryman in the making.

For all of his "all boy" traits, there is another side to Sean. He is a tender, caring person. As a child Sean was not the kind of individual that deliberately hurt animals or humans. When he was nine years old Tom taught him how to use a rifle. He was insistent on Sean learning to respect guns while taking away the mystique of guns through target practice. Sean enjoyed target practice and got it into his head that he wanted to go hunting. He was relentless with Tom. The thing about Sean is that once he gets an idea into his head, he doesn't let it go. Sean didn't understand the true ramifications of hunting. Tom, whose thoughts are always on safety, thought that if he didn't take Sean and teach him himself Sean would try it on his own.

On a fall Saturday Tom and Sean went small game hunting. For the greater good Tom sacrificed a chipmunk. He shot the chipmunk but didn't kill it right away. Tom walked Sean to where the chipmunk was suffering to show him what it meant to kill a living, breathing creature. After that day Sean's only interest in shooting was target practice. Tom and Sean have shared that interest ever since.

The chipmunk lesson was difficult for a nine year old; however, it was important to teach Sean about guns, bullets and the finality of pulling the trigger. He disliked watching the chipmunk die and to this day does what he can to alleviate the suffering of animals and people around him. In high school he became a volunteer fireman because he had a desire to help people in distress. When he watched his country endure the pain of 9/11 he felt it was right to fight for those who no longer could.

There was only one time in our life together that I seriously worried that we wouldn't be able to feed, clothe and house our family. Tom had become seriously ill with encephalitis. He was unable to work and had filed for disability benefits. The insurance company was doing all they could to NOT pay his claim and dragged out the process for many months. Up until then it was the most difficult period of our lives. We were followed and photographed, our garbage was picked through and we were constantly on the defensive. Were it not for financial help from my brother we would have lost our home. At the time I did not have the education or work experience to get a decent paying job. I disliked knowing that I couldn't provide a sustainable income for my family. This scare was the catalyst for me to return to college and earn my bachelors degree. Never again would I allow myself to be in this kind of humiliating position. I felt a personal empowerment and a quiet confidence grow through my studies.

During the period of waiting for a final decision from the insurance company we had one of the snowiest winters on record with school closing for almost the entire month of January. The kids were nine and ten years old at the time. They did their best to help me shovel the snow but they didn't really make a dent in the mounds that were falling. Tom was, for the most part, upstairs in bed with an IV of antibiotics. He had massive headaches and constant fatigue. He, too, was unable to help me shovel the snow. When I was out shoveling the isolation was a relief. It gave me the needed time and opportunity to yell and scream with no one around to hear me. As a family we were suffering in so many ways yet we never gave up on each other; we became stronger as a result of the challenges we faced.

Almost every night the kids and I brought Tom dinner and ate with him in the bedroom on a card table. We watched movies with him and read books together. Tom often made us laugh when we didn't feel like it. The kids were close to Tom and didn't like seeing him in this condition. Tom and I told them everything we knew about his illness and because of this I believe they weren't frightened. Tom would become permanently and totally disabled by the disease and would eventually win his disability case. He has been disabled for more than ten years and the damage from the disease continues to haunt us, sometimes when we least expect it. It would play a role in how we felt about Sean and the war, increasing the stress in our lives substantially.

Laughing uproariously while on their first visit to the Pacific Ocean.

Doing homework was one of Sean's least favorite after school activities.

Tom giving Sean his first firearm safety lesson.

Preparing to bath themselves in mud.

II.

9/11: The Awakening

Sean graduated from Cornwall high school in June 2001. Cornwall is located 60 miles north of New York City, and ten miles north of West Point in the Hudson Valley. He wasn't terribly interested in high school and he couldn't wait to graduate. Two of his favorite activities when he was a senior in high school were that of fireman and a course in community policing offered through a town program. These are what kept him interested and motivated enough to finish high school and move on.

Sean loved being a fireman. It was his first introduction to men doing hard, meaningful work. When we would hear the fire alarm sound in the middle of the night, we knew Sean would be barreling out of bed and down the stairs in seconds. I don't think he missed one fire call.

In September 2001 Sean enrolled in a community college three hours north of us, sharing an apartment with two friends Tom Smith, who he met in high school and John Albarino, who had been Sean's friend since fourth grade. During high school the three of them had been volunteer firemen. Sean and his two buddies had similar plans. John was interested in pursuing a career with the New York City fire department, Tom's goal was to be a paramedic and Sean was looking forward to joining a police force.

Together the three roommates watched the horror of 9/11 unfold on TV in their fourth floor walk-up apartment in

Herkimer, New York. They would drive as close to New York City as they could to offer their help, however, by the time they reached the city it was closed off to all but professional rescuers. It was a surreal time for all Americans and no less so for them. As young adults they have had terrorism imposed on them in a personal way. They were devastated.

John, Tom and Sean the three high school buddies turned college roommates attended many memorial services of fallen firemen for months after 9/11. The following are some of the firemen from our area Orange County, New York who lost their lives on that fateful day:

Asaro, Carl Firefighter (F/F), Battalion 9, Middletown, NY
Atlas, Greg Lt, Engine 10, Howells, NY
Barnes, Matthew F/F, Ladder 25 Monroe,NY
Devlin, Dennis Battalion Chief, Battalion 9,
    Washingtonville,NY
Giordano, John F/F, Ladder 37, Newburgh, NY
Hamilton, Robert F/F, Squad 41, Washingtonville, NY
Kumpel, Kenneth F/F, Ladder 25, Cornwall, NY
Marino, Kenneth F/F, Engine 33, Monroe, NY
Montesi, Michael F/F, Rescue 1, Highland Mills, NY
Nevins, Gerard F/F, Rescue 1, Campbell Hall, NY
Perry, Glenn Lt, Ladder 25, Monroe, NY
Ruback, Paul F/F, Ladder 25, Newburgh, NY
Van Hine, Richard "Bruce" F/F, Squad 41, Greenwood
    Lake, NY
Weis, David F/F, Rescue 1, Maybrook, NY
Whitford, Mark F/F, Engine 23, Salisbury Mills, NY

The boys attended the services in their dress uniforms as members of their volunteer fire department. The impact of these funerals on Sean was extraordinary. He changed the course of his life and has not looked back since. In fact, his decision would challenge me in ways I didn't know possible.

*Tom, Sean and Erik Kukkonen
taking a break while on one of
our Cape Cod vacations.*

*John is hanging an American flag
outside their college apartment days after 9/11.*

*John (left) and Sean (right)
participating in a Student
Against Drunk Drivers
demonstration at the end of
their high school senior year.*

Left to right: Tom Smith, John, Sean and Erik in a photo op at the Hudson River Park in Cornwall before the senior prom. (Although Erik didn't go to the prom he came to see them off).

Tom, John and Sean on graduation day.

Sean (left) and John Albarino (right) after the May, 2001 Cornwall Memorial Day parade.

III.

PATRIOTISM

MY "ALL BOY" WAS GROWING UP. In the spring of 2002 after his freshman year of college Sean joined the Army. He would spend most of the summer in Cornwall with us, working as a lifeguard and hanging around with his friends. He reported for duty the end of August 2002.

I was unaware that he was going to enlist until June 6, 2002. Tom was the one to tell me. Good move! I doubt I would've handled it well if Sean had been the one to tell me. Tom broke the news to me at breakfast. He took me to a public place to minimize my reaction recognizing that by the time we left the restaurant I would have processed the information enough to cope.

A few days after Tom shared the enlistment news the recruiter came to the house in the early evening to go over the details of the contract. I'm not sure but I think I cried all day at work. At the time, I was working for a person that was not very kind and who took every opportunity to attack when she saw signs of weakness. Well, she slammed me that day. I was hurting to the core and she just kept on hitting with nasty comments. By the time I got home my eyes were swollen. I was embarrassed to have to meet the recruiter looking like I did. I didn't want Sean to know I was crying about his enlistment so I told him work had been unpleasant that day.

I think I was unnerved by Sean's enlistment because I had a sense this was going to be big. We had troops fighting in

Afghanistan and there was talk on the news of a military build-up in Kuwait.

I was struggling at work as I had been charged with closing community programs that served the elderly, telling people I supervised that they no longer had a job and grappling with being moved under a vice president whose disposition on most days was nasty and cutting to anyone who didn't jump high enough for her. It was time for me to move on and look for a new job. Our plan was to look for a job in the south where the weather would be kinder to Tom's aching body. With Sean leaving in August for a three-year enlistment and Kate going to college in September it seemed as though there couldn't be a better time to move. We were blissfully unaware that we were entering into a traumatic period: an empty nest, a new job, a major move, a daughter struggling with being away at college, a new dimension to an old illness and a son in combat.

The end of the summer was a poignant time for all of us. The town of Cornwall was a wonderful place to raise children. It is a family town with the high school, hospital and fire department in the heart of town. The kids were both lifeguards in the town and seemed to know every one. It was to be a difficult move for Kate and for us. Kate was going off to college for the first time and I accepted a position at Duke University Eye Center in Durham, North Carolina. Sean, on the other hand, was having the adventure of a life time; he was becoming an infantryman, a life size GI Joe!

The letters Sean wrote during basic training and Operation Iraqi Freedom inspired me to share them. Sean's letters as well as those of all who had been in the war, and continue to serve where there is conflict, are important elements of our country's history. The letters serve to never let us forget that a troop is a human being not a statistic; they are brothers and sisters, husbands and wives, fathers and mothers, daughters and sons. As a mother of a soldier and with the blessing of my family I decided to share the letters our son and Kate's brother wrote to us. They serve as a reminder that our soldiers and their families are deeply invested in the decisions made by our government to go to war.

Every time a soldier is injured or dies a vigil of waiting begins anew. While Sean was in Iraq I often struggled with these kinds of questions: Is someone going to come to my door tonight to tell me it was my son? How soon would I know? Did the unspeakable happen to my son? Did the reporter say the soldier was from the 3rd Infantry? The questions were endless. I ask these things of myself but was afraid to voice them out loud. Finding out that it wasn't my son sent a terrible flood of relief through every fiber of my being. Knowing that it was another mother's son and that she would be the one to suffer the night, sent waves of guilt washing over me. It is for all of us who have experienced war, directly or indirectly that we have chosen to share our letters, our story.

Sean's letters are a testament to his love of family and the closeness he feels to us. He wrote enthusiastically while in basic training and shared his deepest thoughts during the war, the most difficult and challenging time of his young life. My "all boy" was growing up.

The first set of letters is from Sean while he was in basic training. It was a busy time for us due to the move and job change. We hadn't sold our house in New York yet and we didn't have a forwarding address to give Sean before he left for basic training. I was overwhelmed with the reality that we would literally be out of touch with him until the Army gave him permission to contact us. Naturally, I wondered how all that would work since he wouldn't have our new address or phone number until the Army decided it was time to let him read our letters.

At the same time we were engrossed in getting Kate ready for her first year of college. She was having a difficult time saying goodbye to her friends, girls she had known since she was in the third grade, and to the home she had known for years. Tom and I dropped Kate off at school; our hearts broke as she wept uncontrollably. We were very quiet on the way home as we both knew we would emotionally cave in if we spoke a word.

Days later we received our first letter from Sean. It was short and to the point yet Sean was already beginning to exhibit a flare for getting his message across in writing. In a few short lines, written on a 3 x 5 piece of paper, he conveyed that he was doing well and he missed us. Its funny how we drank in those few words and how good we felt. We knew he was going to be okay.

> *August, 2002:*
> *Mom + Dad,*
> *It is day one of my official training. I have next to no time to write right now so I'm going to send you my address – please give it to everyone who will want it.*
> *If there is a true emergency contact the Red Cross, they will notify me. More letters will follow soon:*
> *Address*
> *PFC Ward, Sean Thomas RN*
> *447 FCo 2/58 Infantry*
> *9375 Conway Dr*
> *Ft. Benning, GA 31905-5914*
> *Follow it to the letter please as is on my return address. I love you and write me a lot.*
> *Its Extremely Hard but I like it.*
>
> *PFC Ward*
> *XXOO*
> *P.S. Phones are earned you know?*
> *P.P.S. I miss you guys*

Come September we had to put ourselves in high gear. We had a lot to do before we moved to North Carolina not the least of which was finding suitable interim housing until our house in New York sold and we bought a new house in Durham. We made a quick real estate trip south and hooked up with a fantastic realtor, Debbie White. Debbie quickly took us under her wing. She showed us many good neighborhoods to consider when we were ready to buy but more importantly she helped us find an apartment. There was no financial incentive for her help with our apartment search just her incredible kindness, which we greatly appreciated. She gave us first hand experience with southern hospitality. Debbie would later be one of our greatest Durham supporters during the war.

On the way home from the real estate trip I kept my sunglasses on and turned my head to look out the window for the entire ride. I was sad to be leaving our home in New York and all that was familiar to my kids and me. The tears streamed down my cheeks. There was nothing I could do to stop them. I didn't want Tom to know I was crying. They were secret tears. I didn't want him to try and rationalize my sadness away. Deep down I was scared and resistant to so much change so quickly. I couldn't share that with him. We had moved a few times in our life together, it wasn't something I enjoyed doing. It was a lot of work and took me out of my comfort zone. The fact that we were moving because of my job made things more difficult for me. I had never moved because of my job before, so I had always had the time to do all the things that needed to get done when moving from one state to another. In reality the act of moving is just one long list of details that need to be attended to, I wasn't in the mood for them. I was missing my kids and the life I once knew.

Receiving letters from the kids became the highlight of my week. Kate would email me or we would instant message each other and Sean would write. Sean's letter often came just in time, when I was really missing him. The letters felt like long distance hugs.

September 8, 2002
Mom,

Hi Mary. How are things back at the house? How's Portia? How's work? Its Sunday here, my second one and locker inspections are tomorrow so things are tense. Work here is hard, very hard. The food is good and we eat enough so that's always a plus.

I went through the gas chamber Sunday correction, last Wednesday. That was the scariest moment of my life. I couldn't help but think that that moment was going to be the end of my life. I had prepped for death and was willing to accept it. The second we took our gas masks off I started to choke, and that's when I thought it was all over. Then we got the signal to clear out, and I did. I lived, what an amazing thing! I was so happy. In fact I went in again w/o a mask again just to be tough guy! Wouldn't you know I was the only guy in the whole Company that went back for more. My reward was a donut. All that for a jelly donut.

I don't have any more time to write right now and I only have one stamp left so if you could send some stamps in the mail that would be great, so I could write some more. I got your last letter by the way, and I tear up every time I read it. Just seeing your handwriting makes me feel great, thanx. Keep em comin.

Love,

Sean

P.S. Tell dad I start B.R.M. Monday: Basic Rifle Marksmanship. I get to qualify.

At the time Sean wrote the following letters we were packing up the house. I had to report for my new job on October 7th. We had a lot to do to get ready for moving day not the least of which was securing a buyer.

We also had to sell Sean's car, a '92 Camaro he rescued and resurrected. A car he loved and was hoping we would keep for him. Every time he pulled up to the house in the car our dog, Portia, would go crazy barking in the house or on the porch. She has always been crazy about him! When we were selling the car we would drive it once in a while just to keep it running well and Portia would flip every time we pulled up to the house.

When she'd realize it was us she would look us up and down and walk away in disgust.

Unfortunately for him we weren't able to take the car with us. It had already cost a lot in repairs so we were happy when we sold it for a decent amount that he could put toward a new car when he graduated from training.

It was also Kate's first week at college and away from home. She traditionally has not done well with big life changes. This was to be a stressful week for her that included celebrating her 18th birthday essentially amongst strangers. Particularly since she has always enjoyed our family birthday parties!

I was winding down my job and decided to take the day off to spend it with her. We invited her friend from home, Alaina, who was also Sean's girlfriend at the time, to take the 8 hour round trip with us to have a birthday lunch with Kate. Alaina was quite a trooper for joining us! Kate was as thrilled to see us as we were to see her, but leaving was gut wrenching. We all knew we wouldn't see each other again until Thanksgiving. The day before Thanksgiving was graduation day for Sean. It was going to be a long stretch for all of us.

> *Saturday, September, 14, 2002*
> *Hey Kate,*
>
> *Your letters really cheer me up, keep writing. Its difficult for me to find time to write to everyone and any one at all. I actually forgot it was your b-day so happy belated birthday Bam. It's so busy here but today is the first day I get off what we call total control which means we get treated more like human beings so that's always nice.*
>
> *How are things there? Meet any guys yet? Did you see Alaina and the girls for your b-day? Well have fun either way. Today I was selected to run in a two mile team formation for the Patriot games, a big event like a mini Olympics. I ran it in 13:42 sec's. A personal best by far, and good enough for*

third place. Our company, Foxtrot – the Wildcats,
got first place overall and won a huge trophy. It was
our first taste of real fun since we been here, it was
great. I get one phone call tomorrow so I'm going to
call home and Alaina's, I hope they are there b/c it
could be a month before I use the phone again.

Any way, just keep writing b/c mail is what
cheers up the GI. So Love you and hope to hear
from you soon.

Love,
Sean
P.S. Happy Birthday
GO ARMY!

• • •

14 Sept 2002
Hi Mom,

I got your letter that you first sent me, it was
pretty much identical to the first one so nothing
new. Whats new? You quit your job by now proba-
bly. How's the dog, dad, and any offers on the house
yet? You got good money for my car so that's good.
Today was our first day of freedom, so we can listen
to music, eat as much as we want and sleep all day,
its great!

You should send me a picture of our family. So I
can look at it, that would be nice. I got two letters
from Kate already, and I wrote my first one to her
this Sat. Her B-day was yesterday and we were
supposed get a phone call privilege but it was moved
to today, so I hope you guys are home. I sent one let-
ter to SSG Nelson just to tell him whats up. O yeah
I ran 2 miles in 13:42 yesterday! Dad will know
the whole story it was great.

So things are going great, my self esteem is

returning and I'm getting lean and mean. Tell Grandma's & Grandpa's I said I love them, I had to throw their address out so I don't have them, but tell them when you get a chance. Ok Mary, I love you. Do good things.

Love,
Sean

• • •

14 September 2002
Hey Dad,

Its Saturday the 14th and we passed our phase one inspection which means we get off total control today. We get more responsibility and the DS isn't on our ass so much.

Things are going good here, however, I did find that we are not Hells Kitchen, that's the 1/19. We are House of Pain – just as bad haha! Our Platoon name is the Road Dawgs and when called to attention in the morning we sound off w/

Foxtrot Infantry
Blood thirsty war machines
Ready to fight ready to kill
Ready to die but never will

Rangers through the night
Lead the way to the fight
Wading through the blood they spill
Airborne Rangers kill at will

Airborne in the sky, faces painted as they fly
Dropping low and killing fast, now its time to
Kick some ass.
Foxtrot 2.......5.......8..........Infantry
Wildcats!!!

We shout that at the top of our lungs and its great, I like that motto. Today was one unbelievable day man, we had these Patriot Games today. The Pat. Games are Battalion size and we compete w/in the Batt b/w Co's. I got selected to run in the 2 mile run b/c I ran my first APFT 2 mile run in 15:40 min. So I was excited.

When it came time to run, I heard we run in an eight man formation w/a 1Lt leading our run. I was nervous b/c I'm not a good runner like that. But I promised the 1Lt that I wouldn't drop out – what a shithead I knew I couldn't keep up w/those guys, what was I thinking?!

It was the most difficult thing I could have done all basic training long, but w/the other guys pumping me up and getting me to go harder, I finished. I said, shit man, that sucked, and then the time results came in, and I ran that shit in 13:42!!! Can you believe that?! What a great day.

Tomorrow and the rest of today we get to do nothing b/c the Wildcats won all the events, or most of them anyway, and all day tomorrow – nothing. It was a great feeling b/c the whole Batt. hates us b/c the guys who have been here for 10 – 12 weeks lost to us who have been here for 3 weeks haha! More Pride!

I wrote Kate today b/c I forgot bout her B-day so o well and Tues we get pull the trigger fun stuff.

I get to make a phone call tomorrow so I hope you guys are home. Man some of these pussy's are still crying – Babies about home. But I'm good cause I want to be here, you know. Ok so I'm gonna split and write mom tomorrow, so keep working out and eatin right – cause lord knows I have to. Speaking of Lord – todays the first day I missed church – I'm getting back into that. Good Stuff.

> *Alright talk to you tomorrow hopefully. So*
> *down a few for me ok? Love you guys.*
> *Wildcats,*
> *Shoot Straight Sean*

Sean did call us that weekend, though he didn't have much time to talk. The Army is good at timing phone calls. Even when he was in Kuwait and Iraq his phone calls were timed. More often than not all we did was listen to what he had to say. We had very little opportunity to respond to him. I believe we managed to tell him we would be moving soon and the new address and phone number would be coming in a letter to him.

Sean didn't have our new address yet so the next few letters took a few days longer to reach us. The post office in Cornwall received the letters first and then they forwarded them on to our new address. Since he didn't have our new phone number either we were in a black out period.

Sean sent the following letter to tell his dad that he would be qualifying in a few days. They were both excited about it.

> *September 23, 2002*
> *Hey Dad,*
>
> *Mon I had a bad shooting day. But it wasn't just me my whole company shot like shit, and I was one of only eleven of my platoon that qualified. I should clarify, I was hitting every target, nearly, and then my rifle jammed up like the piece of shit it is. I hate that fucking thing. I could fire that god damn SKS all day, not clean it for two days, and that bitch could hit a dime at 200 hundred yards.*
>
> *I have learned really good fundamentals here and I know I can qualify expert. Whats going to stop me is my rifle double feeding. I have to clean that thing so well, which I did today and the true test is going to be Thursday. I get to practice again Wednesday, so we'll see how well I cleaned it.*

I just got your letter you sent from 15 Sept. and I figured I would write back cause I got some my pen is running out of ink, sorry. Ok good now, I got some down time and ahhhhh! Stupid pen! Ok, my third pen now. Anyway we got a six mile road march tomorrow and it shouldn't be so bad.

Your gone this week anyway so since we got formation in 5 min I'm gonna split.

See ya,
Sean

Tom was thinking about Sean all week. He was just itching to find out how he had done on the range. It was something they talked about for months prior to the event. Sean use to lie in bed at night planning how he would succeed at this. He had little academic interest in most areas except when it came to shooting. He studied the subject to the point where his conversations about guns, bullets and trajectories were incomprehensible to me. He was passionate in his approach to learning all he could about the subject.

Sean's MOS (military occupational specialty) was Infantry, both he and his father knew that shooting well was essential. However, I was just beginning to understand the importance of it and it would be a while before I truly embraced the significance. Sean and his dad didn't know for sure that he would see conflict; however, with all that was happening in the world it was difficult not to see it coming. Shooting well enough to qualify expert was a goal that would eventually have real application.

The results of qualifying are divided into the following categories:

Unqualified
Marksman
Sharpshooter
Expert

Sun 29, 2002
Hey Dad,

Yesterday I got a pass, as a platoon we all went down to the Rec Center for 4 hours to utilize the phones. We got our pass, at least those who Qualified did, at the end of BRM (Basic Rifle Marksmanship). Man what a challenge. It was Thursday and we arrived at the range at about 0600 and it was foggy out. So I was just telling myself to relax the fog will lift, right. So as we wait for the other platoons for about 2 hours the fog thins out and eventually leaves, what a relief. But if you were to look up at the sky you could see the clouds move across the sky like crazy, and that's when the wind started to kick up, and a light drizzle began to fall.

It started to rain. I said great, you know, here I am, I know for a fact I can hit all forty of forty targets that pop up and Qualify expert and of course it's raining. From where I was standing behind the Berm waiting in line to shoot I had a good view of down range. I could see the measured 300 yard target from where I was standing, which put that target at just under 500 yards. So I said if I can see it at 500 I'll have no problem seeing it at 300. So I drive on.

Time flies by and as your waiting you get to see the other guys come off the range and get their results right then and there. I mean there's a Captain standing there and he shakes your hand and pins it to your chest on the spot. So that's cool. Anyway, you see the results are discouraging b/c many people went UnQ and there were a whole lot of Marksmen. As you probably remember from the Marine Corps almost everything is alphabetical, so I'm in 4 platoon 4 squad Bravo team, last man.

But that's ok I suck it up and drive on.

So where was I? O right. Ok now what that means is that I had a long wait before it was my turn to fire. I was in firing order 13. So there's twelve ranks of a 9 man front ahead of me. Each man has two magazines of 20 rounds. He has to fire from a foxhole, and in the prone unsupported firing positions, at a target that pops up from three to five seconds. So basically I had a long and boring wait, but I drive on.

Its about two o'clock in the afternoon and its my turn. I get the command to lock the bolt to the rear and present arms. Then my firing order, file out on to the range. I get assigned to foxhole 10. In front of my position is one other shooter. He gets to shoot and then its my turn. So of course I'm doing a lot of pacing by now b/c I'm watching the guy in front of me shoot in near hurricane weather and he sucks, and there's another platoon's drill sergeants watching me, but that's ok I'm gonna drive on.

Then the guy in front of me gets the command to clear the foxhole and clear the firing line. Then the command comes for me to move forward get into a good supported firing position, adjust my sandbags as needed and get ready to go. Followed closely behind the command to secure one 20 round magazine and lock and load. I do that. Move the selector switch from safe to semi. Right side is clear, left side is clear, center is clear. Firers fire when ready!

25m-kill, 50m-kill, 100m-kill, 175, 250, 275, kill, hit, hit, kill, hit. Miss…I missed the first three, three hundred yard target that popped up. There's four 300 yard targets that pop up total. I missed the first one and it disappointed me. However, I drive on, shrug it off, continue. I'm confident I at least Qualified, so that's good. One thing I forgot to men-

tion was that when we were told to lock and load, I slammed the magazine in too hard and one round popped out. I thought o shit, that's going to be the deciding round. No time to pick it up and place it back in the magazine. I drive on.

I get the command to clear the foxhole, move to the right and get into the prone unsupported firing position. As I do that I quickly pick up the rogue round and place it into my second magazine, and get in to position. By now its raining pretty damn hard and rain keeps getting into the rear aperture of my M16 A4 and visibility is almost not there, but I am infantry and drive on.

Blow the water out of the sight and wait for the next target to pop up so I can blow his tiny little head off. The next 3, 300 yard targets pops up and I don't fire, why? B/c the enemy is less of a threat at 300 then at 50 or 25 yards away. In the army we shoot against multiple targets, like 150 yd and a 300 will pop up. If you miss the 150 refire at it and let the 300 go. Because you get issued one round target so you have to conserve and be accurate. It was particularly difficult because I was freezing wet and cold, but in combat the grunt doesn't choose the time or the place, so I drive on. I get to the end, I know cause I'm counting rounds, two left. Two targets pop up. A 250, and a 100 yard target. I nail the 100 center mass, I adjust, find the 250 and for some reason I almost didn't fire, I think I was thinking that there was no way I shot expert so I was going to let it go. I didn't, I plinked the bastard in the forehead. Its over, I'm done now. Eject the magazine and wait for the orders.

I'm told to exit the range, and as I'm exiting the range I hear the tower announce the greatest thing I have ever heard. But could I be right? "Lane 10 good job expert" Its true dad. 36 kills, one miss and the rest I let go to play it safe. Expert. What a beautiful thing. It truly was the greatest thing I have ever heard.

When I was filing off the range was when I get some serious recognition. DS walking around, Captains, 1Lt's, 1 Sgt's running around like chickens w/their heads cut off wanting to know who the private was that Qualified expert was. I got to stand next to the guidon b/c I'm the pride of the Company. Its so difficult to keep your military bearing when all you want to do is holler out and smile all day. Its at that point standing next to my guidon that nothing matters, tork sessions, the fact that it is pouring at this point, that lunch is going to be liquid, it all doesn't matter, and all cause I drove on.

Expert dad. My sole military goal I achieved. In a god damn tropical storm. My rewards were plentiful my friend, countless. From extra food to Main Post pass. However I turned down the pass to hang w/my fire team cause we are a tightly woven death squad! Oh geeze, I forgot to mention why my expertise was so prized in Foxtrot 2/58 INF. You see I'm the only one in the entire company that shot expert. No lie, No fish story 100% the truth. I'm going to get special recognition on graduation day. They call me expert here now, and of course I'm suckin it up People are in awe of me its great.

The good thing was that I had a pass yesterday. The worst thing of all was that I was looking forward to telling you in person yesterday, or what I meant was on the phone, cause I had unrestricted phone use. I didn't know you guys were moving on the 28 b/c the army holds mail the entire week you are on the range, I don't know why, but I couldn't help it, I called but you must have left. But I drive on.

So that's about it. I have you to thank for teaching me good fundamentals. Steady position, aiming, breathing, trigger squeeze. The keys to expert. And I have the Army to thank for setting those principles in stone. And now the expert must go shine some doors knobs hahaha.

I hope you guys are happy in your new place and everything is running smoothly. I hope to God you get this letter in the mail cause there is no way I'm writing this again. Tell Kate I get her mail and to keep writing, time is limited I write when I can to her.

That's all I can think of right now. I'll write again later. Oh I went to the M203 range on Friday and since I shot expert I got to fire live HE rounds instead of dummy grenades. It was awesome! Ok I'll talk later. I'm going to the field this coming Mon for 5 days so I'm not going to write you or receive mail, I think for a week.

Tell Mom I love her and she is, as per usual, allowed to read this letters at your discretion. Love you guys see ya later.

Expert! Can you believe it?!

Love,

Sean

I remember sitting in the car reading the letter after Tom. We were both laughing and crying at the same time. For some reason I tear up when my kids do really well. When they played sports in high school I would tear up when Kate scored in basketball in a difficult situation or when Sean did well in football. It was only natural that I would cry when I read the "expert" letter.

I felt badly that he had tried to call us after we moved. It was one of those details I didn't want to fall through the cracks. I comfort myself with the thought that he wouldn't have written this experience down if he could have reached us by phone.

While Sean was shooting expert and moving on with training we were trying to settle down in our temporary quarters. Neither Tom nor I have ever enjoyed apartment living. Thankfully, by the time we moved we had a buyer for our Cornwall house. It was important to us to find a new home as soon as possible so we began working with our realtor, Debbie White, once again.

Debbie and Tom hit it off well. They were both interested in landscape painting. Tom had spent the better part of the last 10 years learning how to paint; it was to become a lifeline to his sanity while learning to live with his disabilities. The painting was the common bond between Debbie and Tom helping to cement a friendship that continues today.

Within weeks we had settled on a new house in a new subdivision 6 miles from my job. It was a priority that I live close to work, as the parking situation at Duke is terrible. I knew the time it took to park and get to my car had the potential to frustrate me.

In addition, I enjoy my exercise in the morning and was concerned the parking situation would impact my daily routine. The exercise helps me to synthesize stress in my life. The last year had been particularly difficult and I wanted to be sure I didn't miss any of my workouts.

We were excited about the new house. It was partially built when we went contract. The day we negotiated the contract Sean called us on the cell phone. We knew his calls were limited so anytime we left home we forwarded our calls from home to the cell phone. Little did we know we would be call forwarding for the next 9 months! We interrupted the negotiations to give our undivided attention to him.

The next 6 weeks would fly by. We were caught up with house buying details and my new job. Kate was settled in at school by then. Sean seemed to be doing well. I was finally feeling a little more at peace with our world.

The following are letters Sean wrote to Kate and to Tom and me. They are the last two letters from that time period that I could find. I must have lost a few in the confusion of moving from the apartment to the house. If I had known he was going to be in a war the following spring I would have saved every single one of them. I've come to understand we often live our lives that way. We think we have time to do things, to say things, to live without the impending consequences of death. I have every single letter he wrote home from Iraq. Having a son engaged in a war taught me that I may not have a lifetime of loving him that I had to cherish every moment.

> *14 October 2002*
> *Hey Kate,*
>
> *Sorry I haven't written in so long. I ran out of paper, that official paper so now I use this cool loose leaf. I'm glad to hear that you seem to be doing the right thing in college. Just don't forget to have your share of the other though. You earned it in high school. Its important to get good grades as you well know because every body will look at those and pass judgment based on your grades. So do the right thing and you can never go wrong.*
>
> *There's a guy on the other side of the bay that thinks your hot, he's no stud, but not ugly either. His last name is Heather. He's from Missouri. He's cool I like him. But anyway I'm not gonna bring him home I think he wants to marry his girlfriend when he gets out of basic.*
>
> *How's the weather there? Its cold in the mornings here but its like 75 degrees and since I'm used to the hot climate that feels cold to me. The usual afternoon temp is way up in the 90's. I like it though.*
>
> *I excel down here, this is my element I've discovered. I'm in competition right now for honor grad,*

I have to boost my sit ups though. I can run 2 miles in 13:00 min now and do 45 push ups in 2:00 minutes that's pretty good. Do you have a phone #?

If my letters make no sense sometimes its because I don't have time for proper form, I just write what comes to mind.

I have a 8 mile road march coming up this Wednesday so it should be tough w/a 45 pound rucksack and helmet.

Just remember that when things get tough, or if you feel lonely, or if you miss Portia or your friends and Mom & Dad, that I'm in the woods with face paint digging a hole, in a helmet, BDU's and combat boots, with gnats crawling up my wet nose, in my dirty ears, inhaling them, in my eyes. Digging a hole to take a shit in. Pulling 1 hour shifts to watch the perimeter every night, with 3 hours of sleep, sleeping on the hard ground with wild dogs circling the woods at night. Its ok though, I say because I asked for this. I knew things like this would happen. I say to myself, drive on. Drive on and things will get better. Get through the moment. If you do the harder right over the easier wrong, you can never be wrong.

Ok its time to go polish some door knobs now. I'll write as soon as I can make some time too ok? Love you. Have fun. Drive on.

Love brother Sean
P.S. Keep writing
XXOO

Kate read the letter to me over the phone. It didn't faze me at all that he was living in the woods in less than optimal conditions. It was training; it was what he was supposed to do. Once it was over he would be back on post, have a hot shower, food and a bed to sleep in. During the war he wrote a letter home describing similar conditions only this time it was real and none of us knew when or if he would return.

I loved that he wrote this letter to Kate. She was struggling being away from her family. It didn't help that we moved 15 hours south either. She couldn't come home easily and we couldn't go see her on a whim. Sean and Kate were close, they were almost always together, from the time they were old enough to have play dates their friends called them "Sean and Kate", as though they were one unit. Instead of addressing them individually they would ask if Sean and Kate were home even if they just meant to ask for one of them. She missed all of us. Sean uses a part of our family prayer to help her stay the course and encourage her by telling her "If you do the harder right over the easier wrong, you can never be wrong". This is the prayer we said every night before we ate dinner, it is a variation of the prayer the cadets learn at West Point:

> Make us to choose the harder right
> instead of the easier wrong.
> Never to be content with the half truth
> when the whole truth can be won.
> All of which we ask in the name
> of the great friend and master of men,
> Jesus Christ, our Lord.

14 October 2002
Hey Mom & Dad,

Things are going good here, I have one half hour to write so its gonna be short. I've got a 30 hours pass coming up on the 27th of October. I have your new number so I will definitely give you a call.

I hear that you guys like the apartment, so that's good. Hopefully the house will be what you are looking for. I was a church this Sunday, and there was this recruit in the there with his parents,

*and I turned to the guy next to me, that's Byler he's
from Texas, and I said I can't wait for that day to
come. Except than he shattered my dream by telling
me that graduation is on a Wednesday, Ha Ha Ha!*

*Well things are going smooth here. We had a
light work week, and the next is supposed to be just
as easy. On Wednesday there is a 10 mile road
march, but after that, get this, there is a carnival
on Tuesday that we are allowed to go to. A carnival
in the middle of basic training who would have
thought, not me, that's for sure.*

*Our platoon has lost six people already and 12
more are scheduled to go within the next two weeks
due to various reasons. I think its great because
then we are left with the best in the platoon you
know?*

*The only real other development lately is that I
qualified expert in grenades, and my PT score is
rising, oh and I'm the new team leader for Bravo
Team, good shit.*

*Ok, its rack time so if I get to write tomorrow
then I will. How's the family, and that's about it.
Miss you guys, love ya.*

Love,
Sean
P.S. Thanks for the stamps!
XXOO

We were getting excited to see the kids after such a long
stretch. We picked Kate up at the Raleigh-Durham airport at
4:00 p.m. and drove straight through to Ft. Benning Georgia.
All the kennels were booked due to the Thanksgiving holiday so
Portia came with us. When Portia first saw Kate in the parking
lot she cried and whined, she was beside herself with joy. Of
course I felt like doing the same but it would have looked silly
for me to run in circles and howl.

It took almost ten hours to get to the base. We drove straight through and I mean straight through, we overshot Ft. Benning and ended up in Alabama!

There are two parts to graduating from Basic Training: the first day is the Turning Blue Ceremony, specifically for infantryman, and the second day is graduation for all recruits. At the end of the ceremony the families were invited to put the blue infantry cord on their soldier's uniform. It was at this ceremony that Sean was awarded the Expert Rifleman badge.

When the ceremony began the families were sitting on bleachers and the company marched in formation in front of us. They lined up and stood at attention. We thought we saw Sean about ten different times. It's amazing how they all look alike in a uniform. Even when he played football I couldn't tell him apart from other players. Don't uniforms do a good job of taking away the unique characteristics of an individual?

Then three soldiers came over a hill and there he was! Two of the soldiers were recognized for a high level of fitness and Sean was the only one recognized for qualifying as Expert. When they called his name, naturally I cried and the families went crazy honoring him with whistles and applause.

At the ceremony there was a man who videotaped everything and then offered the tape for sale to the families. I found it strange to commercialize the soldiers training milestone. I could see something like this being available during sporting events but at this occasion it just seemed odd. We had gone to see almost every one of the kid's sports games over the years and sometimes we taped games to have as a visual memory; that was different, it was a game. The videotaping of the graduation by a contracted professional seemed out of place. When I fast forward to the war I can see that the video's by the embedded reporters fit right into our culture of over exposure. The embedded reporting would bring the war into our home 24/7. Thousands of us hoped to see our sons or daughters face pass before the camera. Exposure can be both bad and good. It depends on the situation and the individual. Some people were overwhelmed with the footage coming out of Iraq and others found it comforting. Every day I felt differently about the coverage depending on what was reported about the 3rd Infantry Division (mechanized) also known as the 3rd ID. Tom watched it virtually non-stop. It blew me away to watch too much news yet I was edgy when I didn't know what was going on.

After the Turning Blue ceremony we got to spend some time with Sean. Taking advantage of the beautiful day we drove around the base and Sean gave us an informal tour. He was bubbling with enthusiasm about the past few months. Tom, Kate and I couldn't get a word in even if we had wanted to.

The next day was graduation for a number of different companies. It was held on the parade ground to accommodate all who attended. Of course the event was again videotaped. At this point I decided to buy the tapes mostly because Sean and Portia were captured on it!

The graduation was quite a display of soldiers. There were hundreds of them and each company shouted their cadence just as loud as they could. At the end of the ceremony there was a mock battle with Bradley's roaring onto the parade grounds and infantrymen in full combat gear showing their stuff. The loudspeakers erupted with "Bad to the Bone" by George Thorogood competing with the bellow of the Bradley's. Portia damn near lost her insides when they started firing their weapons; she literally did a back flip and then hid under the bleachers. We couldn't tell who got more attention the dog or the soldiers!

We headed back to North Carolina soon after the graduation: Tom and Sean in the front seat, Kate and I in the back seat with Portia laid out across our laps for the better part of 10 hours. For me, life was close to perfect!

For Thanksgiving it was Erik Kukkonen, a good friend of Sean's from high school, and us. Erik was stationed at Ft. Bragg, which is about 75 miles south of Durham. Erik serves with the 82nd Airborne and was not permitted to go home to New York for the holiday. Even though it was a little cramped in the two-bedroom apartment, it was a weekend that worked out well for

Left to right, top to bottom: Sean is recognized for achieving Expert Marksmen just before the start of the Turning Blue ceremony.

Sean lost his debit card the day before Basic Training graduation. Tom looks on as Sean calls the bank to cancel his card. They both like this photograph; every time they see it, they laugh!

Tom putting the Infantry's Blue Cord on Sean.

Sean and Kate shortly after the Turning Blue ceremony.

all of us. Having Erik to share the holiday made us all a little less homesick for Cornwall. By Sunday Kate and Erik both had to leave. It was Sean, Tom and I for the next 3 weeks.

Sean had to do "Home Town Recruiting". This means that after basic training the soldier has an opportunity to go home and work with the recruiter and then he isn't charged leave time. He works with the recruiting office that enlisted him. Only for Sean this wasn't to be the case since we had moved. It was a little confusing to figure out at first but somehow it seemed to smooth out in the end. Sean didn't have any friends in this area to share his very cool stories with which probably took some of the shine off of the process for him.

Tom and I were busy getting the paperwork and inspections completed on the house. Sean was busy with recruiting duties and looking for a car. He found a real beauty about 3 days before we closed on the house. It was a silver Mustang GT, 5 speed, 8 cylinder little beauty with very little mileage. The fact that the payments were within his budget sweetened the deal. The only glitch was that he needed us to co-sign on the loan and therefore had to wait for our closing to be completed.

The day before we were to close on the house North Carolina suffered one of the worst ice storms in history. Power was out for thousands of people. Our apartment was one of the few areas that had power; however, the area that the house was in didn't. Our attorney and realtor broke the bad news that we wouldn't be able to close that day. The power outage was widespread including the County Clerks office. With the computers down new mortgages could not be recorded. Since the movers had other jobs lined up the following week we had to move that day. I decided we were going to stay in the apartment until the house had power so we held a few things back. Coming from upstate New York, where a dozen or more snowstorms was the norm, I didn't understand how unprepared the area was for winter storms. By the end of the weekend I had figured it out!

By this time Sean was sick and tired of not having a car. He was itching to have his freedom and needed us to get it. He needed us to co-sign on his car loan to get the best interest rate. We were not willing to do this until we closed on our mortgage. His anxiety was palpable yet nothing compared to mine. For the second time in that many months I was inundated with moving details.

Once again Debbie White, our realtor, rescued us. She made arrangements with the contractors to allow us to move our belongings to the house even though we hadn't closed. It was Friday and the earliest we could hope for a closing was Monday. We kept some mattresses, a table, 3 chairs, some kitchen equipment and the TV to keep us occupied. We decided to stay in the warm apartment for as long as necessary. Sean bought a Playstation and burned up his brain playing games for 12 hours a day. It was an incredibly boring and tedious weekend for all of us.

By the end of the weekend the house had power, as did the city of Durham. We were able to close on Monday. From the closing we went to the dealership to help Sean with the car loan. Finally, everyone was content and feeling good about their purchases. For us it was the most beautiful home we had ever dreamed of owning and for Sean it was the most awesome vehicle a young guy could have.

Shortly after Sean bought the car he took a road trip to Cornwall. We mapped out the route and he checked in via cell phone. It is a long trip to take alone and we were concerned that it would overwhelm him and that he'd get lost. It's funny now to think of how nervous we were when he left on this road trip considering where he was to go in the near future.

In New York, Sean visited some of his close friends and returned to familiar places he still called home. He was beginning to figure out that it is difficult to successfully return to a home that is no longer there. The night he arrived home he told me he was happy to be in North Carolina and that he was proud of what we'd accomplished and that just in case I didn't know, his dad was his best friend.

It was December 17th and Sean had to leave to report to Ft. Stewart, Georgia, home of the Third Infantry Division (mechanized) by the 18th. We had a mini-Christmas without Kate and missed her terribly. It was the first time in years that I decorated the tree without her. In fact, she would be the first to tell you the job of decorating usually fell to her, as I was taking courses for years and always seemed to be engrossed in papers or exams at that time of the year. Kate is the epitome of Christmas spirit. I definitely didn't enjoy the process without her. She came home the day after Sean left; it was the first time in their lives they hadn't spent Christmas together.

The house looked stark that Christmas. As beautiful as the house was there was very little furniture in it and the few chairs we had for the table were falling apart. The tree stood in one of the many empty rooms, and the lack of family and friends made the house seem even emptier. We hadn't yet met anyone to spend the day with and distance prevented family from easing the day for us. Kate sat on the floor to open her gifts and put on a brave front. We both had cried by the end of the day.

Just to add further to our misery we couldn't find the angel for the top of the tree. Kate had bought it for me years ago. At the time we had been going through a difficult period. Tom was battling encephalitis and I was battling the disability company for him. To lift my spirits I often read angel stories. Kate noticed and bought me a very special angel to put on the top of the tree and watch over us. We used it every Christmas for 9 years but this year we couldn't find it. We tried to buy one to replace it but it didn't come close to our angel in either beauty or sentiment. This past summer when we were cleaning out the garage we found our angel. When we put her on top of the tree this year we decided that not having her on the tree the prior year was an omen of the events the year was to bring. Kate and I have sworn to never lose her again!

IV.

OPERATION IRAQI FREEDOM: COURAGE

THE DAY AFTER CHRISTMAS SEAN CALLED and told us he thought he would be deployed to Kuwait. Most of the soldiers from the 3rd ID were already in Kuwait. He figured he was leaving within a few weeks. As soon as he had a date for deployment we made arrangements to say goodbye to him ....

I was in shock that he was being deployed so quickly. I had fooled myself into thinking the Army would never send a new soldier this green into a potential war zone. I figured he had another good year stateside with additional training before he would be deployed anywhere. I was experiencing internal panic. Only Tom could detect this and made me promise I wouldn't break down and cry when I said goodbye to Sean. He told me I had to be strong for him. So I was, and Tom wasn't. Tom broke up when it came time to hug Sean. I managed to keep it together at least until we were out of sight.

Of course the sweetest piece of the "goodbye" weekend was that Kate was there with us. Sean and Kate hadn't seen each other since Thanksgiving and wouldn't see each other again for 8 months.

Kate would be home with us until the end of January. She was studying interior design and had to work as an intern over the winter break. Between the internship and a quick trip to Cornwall she was busy. However, just like Sean, Kate was beginning to distance herself from Cornwall and the life she had there. It wasn't an easy transition for her. She handled it exceptionally well and in the end has found a new sense of self as a result of all of these changes.

At this time I was also finishing the last semester of graduate school. I was taking the very last course for the master of public administration (MPA) degree. The MPA degree was offered as an on-line program for the first time through Marist College in Poughkeepsie New York. The on-line format allowed me the flexibility to accept a new job without impacting my studies. Although I could have asked for the final semester to be postponed I thought it would be a good distraction. I was wrong. I did finish the course and graduated in May but it was extremely difficult to concentrate and often became an irritation.

During the months of January and February Sean called when he could. He had little patience for the long phone lines and rather than wait he would find times when it was less busy which was the middle of the night for him and the middle of the day for us. Generally that meant I wasn't around to talk to him. One morning, however, our phone rang at 4:00 a.m. It was Sean and the first thing he said was, "Sorry to wake you, I needed to hear my moms voice". I needed to hear his too.

Sean shared with us during this call that he was a machine gunner as a dismount on a Bradley. This means he rode in the back of a Bradley with six to eight infantrymen.

By the end of January I learned from a mutual friend that one of my former co-workers from New York, Jerry Kiernan, had a son deployed to Kuwait. Once we made contact with Jerry it was wonderful for both of us, and our spouses to share thoughts, fears and concerns. We stayed in constant contact by either email or phone.

Our anxiety centered on the declaration of war. The anticipation of war was overwhelming. It consumed nearly every conversation we had with one another. Being able to share this high level of anxiety with the Kiernan's was a blessing. Other people understood yet they weren't as invested as we were. They listened but they didn't feel it deep down in their hearts. Our friendship with the Kiernan's would develop in a way that only war can foster. Jerry and I would talk about the dark side of war: how we would handle the death of our sons, or what life would be like if they suffered a terrible injury; the kind of talk that sounds morbid and negative to other people who are not in the same place as you are yet it served to comfort us at times. We allowed each other to clarify our feelings when necessary without judgment. Fortunately, a majority of the time Jerry, Jerry's wife Vicki, Tom and I had positive thoughts. We took joy in sharing any good news we heard with each other.

Jerry and Tom spoke almost daily after the Centcom briefings. They knew all that there was to know about the war and what they didn't know they researched. Tom became a master at finding any and all articles pertaining to the 3rd ID.

On the morning of February 12th, Sean's birthday, we were watching the morning news show "Fox and Friends" and realized they were doing a live program from Camp New York in Kuwait; the camp where Sean was living. We were searching the crowds of men for him but to no avail. The newscasters were looking for interesting stories among the troops so we tried to contact the studio to ask them to look for him. In fact I emailed them so many times I got in trouble with AOL for spamming. We spoke with Sean shortly after this broadcast and found out he was taking a course at the time in battlefield first aid and wasn't in the vicinity of the Fox production crew.

By the end of February we were closing in on the very real prospect that we would be engaged in war within weeks. During the last phone call we had from Sean he gave us an indication that this would be the last call for a long time. They were heading out in the desert for MOUT training (urban warfare training) and weren't expecting to be in touch with their families for an extended period.

The media was covering the impending war intensely. Tom has always been a news hound and this was to be no exception. Due to the continuous coverage I was acutely aware of where we were heading as a country, it was only a matter of time before we went to war in Iraq. I must admit if my son had not been involved, I would not have been as informed as I was, but the way things were I had a much-heightened sense of awareness.

I felt myself begin to shut out people around me who were not directly concerned about my son's welfare. I missed living in Cornwall where there were many people who knew and loved him and cared about us as a family. There wasn't one person I knew in Durham whose life would be affected if my son was injured or killed in the war. I knew the Durham community would feel sad for us yet there was no one who would sit on our front porch and tell Sean stories. I couldn't share with anyone the personal memories about Sean like the time he and Erik took their inflatable boats down the Moodna Creek after hurricane Floyd and nearly drowned, or the times he and his friends played paintball for hours on end. There was no one to remember these and all of the other memories of Sean that we have and his friends have. In essence there wasn't anyone around us who loved him.

Our extended families live all over the country so we truly had no one to share our fears, worries and concerns with face to face. The one bright spot was that Kate would be home for a week in March.

While Kate was home for spring break one of the girls Sean and Kate knew from St. Thomas of Canterbury School, their elementary school, did an Internet search of Sean's name, the Army and Cornwall. She found a recent picture of him in Kuwait sleeping next to a tent. She emailed it to Kate's friend Virginia who called Kate at midnight to tell her about the picture and where to find it. It was pretty exciting for all of us when we saw the photograph. I emailed it to everyone in my address book. It was the start of something good. Many of the people I emailed it to, emailed it to people they knew and before I knew it people I didn't know were contacting me to let me know they had hung it up in their offices or as the wallpaper on their computer screen. I half expected to walk into someone's home or office that I was meeting for the first time and find it on their computer screen or hanging on their refrigerator.

REUTERS/CHRIS HELGREN

United States Army Private Sean Ward of Cornwall, NY, catches some sleep between urban warfare training sessions in the north Kuwait desert with his Third Platoon, Charlie Company of the 3115 Infantry from Ft. Stewart, Georgia. January 31, 2003.

The photograph was discovered just days before we went to war. We hadn't seen Sean for two and a half months so we feasted our eyes on him. When my sister, Jessica, saw the photo one of the first things she noticed was how dirty his fingers were. His dirty fingers elicit memories of his younger years playing GI Joe in the dirt.

The photograph was taken, January 31, 2003. The unit Sean was with, the 3rd Infantry Charlie Company 3-15 2nd Brigade Combat Team, was based at Camp New York in Kuwait. It was apropos that the Camp he was based in was Camp New York as it was one of four camps named for the state most affected by the September 11 terrorist attacks, it was the state he was from and 9/11 was the reason he decided to serve his country.

By the time we were aware of the photograph he was long gone from Camp New York. The 3rd ID began to move closer to the Kuwait-Iraq border in early March. Once they left Camp NY they were not permitted to call home. Even though I knew this it didn't make it any easier for me. Every night as I lay in bed I prayed for him and for all of our troops and their families. I prayed for strength, wisdom and the ability to courageously face whatever came our way.

President Bush had gone on television March 17th and given Saddam Hussein one more opportunity to come forward. If Saddam didn't comply then he could expect coalition forces to attack Iraq. At that point the world around me began to feel surreal. At work the next morning we had a meeting with about 20 people in attendance. Before it began one of them asked to have a moment of silence in regard to the ultimatum that was given to Saddam. It nearly broke me. I was so choked up I didn't think I was going to make it through the meeting. Unfortunately it was a meeting in which I was a central participant. I had no way out; in the event I broke down I wouldn't be able to leave. I briefly looked across the table at a few of the women I work with and felt their support for me to stay and get on with it. I appreciated their presence enormously and was able to hold back the tears enough to get on with the meeting. I had the sense it was going to be a long time before I could focus on my work with my normal intensity.

Kate, Tom and I needed a distraction so we bought tickets to see a show for the evening of March 19th. For a few short hours we let ourselves get lost in the unreal world of entertainment. It felt good to be interested in something other than the dark clouds of an impending war. We didn't arrive home until 10 p.m. that evening. The moment I was dreading arrived on that evening, March 19th. While we were out President Bush made a televised announcement that the attack on Iraq had begun with air strikes and the ground war was to follow shortly. One of my friends, Michael Cooney, left a message on our answering machine letting us know he was there if we needed him. For the moment I wasn't answering the phone, it was too difficult to talk to people as I was captured by the images of NBC's David

Bloom riding on an armored vehicle into Iraq with the 3rd ID.

Kate watched the news with us. You can't believe it is happening right in front of you. The things that go through your mind are endless. I wondered how it would feel to watch a bomb drop on a bunch of our Bradley fighting vehicles, knowing that my son might be in one of them. Or how I would feel if a chemical weapon was launched on our troops and Sean was one of them. It would be hours before I would know if it was him yet I would know retrospectively that I had watched it happen. It was macabre.

While I was watching the war unfold I felt proud of my son, the infantryman. I began to wonder what Sean was thinking, what was going through his mind as he sat in a Bradley. Did he know how massive it looked to see the 3rd ID cross the border into Iraq? Could he hear the sounds of weapons being fired? Could he see anything at all? Did it feel the way he thought it would? Was it hot in the back of a Bradley? Was he scared? I was scared for him. I realized I would be scared for a long time.

The next day, March 20th, was my dad's 73rd birthday. I remember thinking that I hadn't sent him a gift or a card. I hadn't been focused on much of anything for a few days. I did call him and we talked, mostly about the war and where we thought Sean might be. My dad then told me my oldest brother had just sent him and my mother a really nice gift. It was a large sum of money that they were just to have fun with. My brother John had done well financially the past year and was sharing some of his happiness and rewards with them. Yet it was really odd for me to hear this on that particular day. My son, their grandson, was in the most violent place on earth. At the time I didn't have room in my life to share in other people's happiness. I was consumed with the war and possibility of chemical and/or biological weapon attacks on our troops; everything else seemed insignificant. I knew they felt the tension of the situation but yet, at the same time their son was sharing a wonderful moment in his life, mine was at war. I wondered why they didn't realize how intense my emotions were. Then it came to me. It wasn't possible for them to know because neither of their sons had been in the military. They had no reference for my experience.

That day I also called in sick. I couldn't deal with people wondering how I was doing. I needed to catch my breath. I hadn't slept well and when I woke up there IT was on television again. If we didn't have MSNBC on we had Fox News on. It was war 24/7, it was great and it was awful. By afternoon Kate and I went to Walmart to get away from all the news and wouldn't you know that every television in almost every aisle was tuned to the war. I never realized that Walmart had that many TV's. As hard as we tried we just couldn't escape the war that day. Thankfully for us we have a good sense of humor and eventually found ourselves laughing at the picture of us trying to find solace in, of all places, Walmart.

The country was becoming more patriotic by the moment. Even at the Walmart checkout there were four men behind us in line each with a hat or t-shirt declaring their Veteran's status. People were hanging yellow ribbons on their doors and mailboxes. American flags were everywhere. After 9/11 people all over the country showed their patriotism by flying the flag on their houses, cars and by wearing flag pins. We were seeing it all over again. People put stickers on their cars that said "We Support Our Troops". When people I didn't know found out I had a son in Iraq they asked me to tell him thank you from them.

During this period I didn't discuss my thoughts on whether or not I believed in what our country was doing. What I will say is that my husband Tom has taught me the absurdity of the question of whether or not we are for the war. He says, and I agree, that war is never a good thing. Every single day I think of the American and Iraqi moms whose sons have died as warriors for their respective countries. When we have to resort to violence in an attempt to find peace something has gone terribly wrong with the process.

The first letter we received from Sean after the war began was dated March 2, 2003. It was postmarked March 13 and we actually received it sometime around March 27th. The letters

took a long time to get to him from us and from us to him. It
would be this way right up until the end of his deployment. It
was frustrating to have the delay in mail. There was no communication for weeks. It seemed like an interminable amount of
time. By the time we read Sean's letter we felt dehydrated of his
presence in our life.

March 2, 2003

*It's the second day now. I was in the track that
was selected to be the courting party for third platoon before we moved to the desert. Yesterday we set
up a shower point, dug a Latrine trench, and set up
concertina wire to protect our position.*

*It won't be long now before I return home. I can
just tell. Either through Baghdad or President Bush,
in fact I would be surprised if I'm here any longer
than one more month.*

*Today is March 02, 2003. Yesterday is the sec-
ond time we have moved from one location to
another. The first was from PA to NY, now its from
NY to a BAA. A BAA is a Brigade Level Assembly
Area. From here we will eventually move from the
BAA to the TAA, Task Force, to a AA. The AA is
where we'll be for no more than two days and then
we start combat operations. That'll give you an idea
of whats goin on.*

*I'm not doing much out here just sittin around
contemplating life making sure my equipment is
functional and ready. Two days ago I got a short
barrel for my M249 Saw, and a sight called the
Elcan M145 w/a 3/5 power telescoping ability, its
fixed power but it doubles my point target range
from 600m to 1200m so naturally I love it. My
Saw is condensed to just over two feet in length,
which makes it very small and even more agile
w/the collapsible buttstock.*

I bought an Advantix camera and all the film in the PX, which is about 7 rolls of film, plus it comes w/one roll. I'm taking pics of lots of things to send home.

Landscape wise there's not much to see, but you've been to the desert and you know. I've got pictures anyway. Its absolutely freezing at night and hot during the day. Not a cloud in the sky hardly ever. Its rained only twice but it rained good. I've been in three sand storms and those aren't pretty.

As the day goes on and the rest of the Brigade and Task Force moves in you sit and watch the Cobras, Hueys, Chinooks, Blackhawks, Sea Stallions, Longbow Apaches, Kiowas, and F16 and F18 Hornets fly overhead. Then on the ground you look out in front of you and see the paladins move in and the Abrams move in, it truly is an awesome sight. When you see a platoon not even a company size element of Bradley's rollin past you it makes you weak in the knees, w/the 25mm cannon the Tow Antitank missile launcher and the 7.62 machine gun Co Ax, and then you think that damn, there's 8 people in the back just armed to the teeth ready to dismount. The sound alone should scare the piss out of the bastards that don't give up.

On a lighter note, I asked Jen out two days before we rolled out. She's great and I can't wait for you guys to meet her. Our relationship has grown out here, its kind of ironic that in such a desolate place where there are no trees and you see more dung beetles than human beings, that you can find love out here. It helps you keep your sanity when you can talk intimately about life with a person who sees things differently. Jen goes to the promotion board in two months, which means she could smoke me, can you believe that?!

Well its 1508 and I'm gonna go dream of the finer things in life, and none of them are in Kuwait. I'm itchin for the mission, I hope it comes soon. I keep one of the letters both you and mom wrote to me in my body armor, and one of the letters that Jen sent before she came here. If we roll north I'd like to keep some of my favorite things closest to my heart.

I'm always thinking of you guys and Kate, and I'm gonna be so excited when the day comes that we can fly out of here. I'll write again some other day. Enjoy the luxuries of life while I can't.

Love you guys.
Sean

The day we received the letter Tom was not home. He was out burning off some energy at Handgunners Inc., the indoor shooting range he joined. This was a good place for him to hang around with men who were supportive, down to earth individuals. Mike Hinshaw, the owner, has been a great supporter of all of the troops and never failed to ask Tom about our son.

It was my day to come home from work and have some time to myself. We were on the look out for a letter from Sean but had no idea when or if we would get one. I was shocked when I opened the mailbox to find a letter from him. I started screaming in the street, jumping up and down with no one around to share it with. I couldn't believe it. I must have looked so silly. There wasn't a soul around and here I was screaming at the top of my lungs. I was overcome with joy. By the time I finished reading it I fell apart. All of the emotion I had bottled up came pouring out.

Since Tom wasn't home I called Kate, my parents and Tom's parents; I read the letter to each of them. Each time I read it I was overwhelmed again. Until then, I had no idea that I had been so tightly wound up.

It was at this time I developed the habit of composing group emails – one for family and one for friends. They were concerned about his safety and this seemed to be the best method of communicating. It served the purpose of keeping them informed without my feeling the need to make multiple phone calls.

By the time we got this letter we had already seen some heavy battles on TV and knew the 3rd ID had been engaged in heavy combat. We had seen the NBC coverage of the incident in which the helicopter Brian Williams, his producer Justin Balding and General Dowling (retired) were traveling in when it was shot at and made an emergency landing. Fortunately for them a 3rd ID platoon had been in the area to provide protection. Protection they would need for nearly three days due to hostile fire and a wicked sandstorm. Little did we know our son's platoon was the one providing protection; it was one of those situations that we would only know the details retrospectively.

In the days before we received Sean's first letter the following occurred: one helicopter was shot down and two crewmen became the first prisoners of war; the 101st Airborne had been attacked in Kuwait by a disgruntled American soldier; the 507th Maintenance Company took a wrong turn that turned deadly with 13 men and two women missing; and we suffered our first casualty. It was an intense period. At home we were on eggshells all of the time.

Tom and I had discussed how we would handle the press if Sean became a casualty. We knew from watching the news that once the name of the soldier was made public the press would try to interview the family. Neither one of us had the desire to publicly air our grief.

Our former local newspaper from Orange County, New York, The Times Herald Record was interested in stories about the local troops who were deployed. Jerry Kiernan called the reporter to tell her about his son Specialist William Sean Kiernan. He called me and asked if it was all right to give her my name and number for an interview about our Sean. In this situation I was happy to participate and interviewed over the telephone on March 26th. The story was published on March 31, 2003:

Excerpt:
FROM HERE TO THERE: STORIES OF OUR LOCAL TROOPS

U.S. Army Spec. William Sean Kiernan and Pfc Sean Ward, 3rd Infantry, 2nd Brigade

Their parents hope they've bumped into each other by now.

It would be comforting to know their sons could be hometown touchstones for each other on the front lines in Iraq.

But it's hard for Jerry Kiernan and Mary Ward to know for sure if their sons, William Sean and Sean, respectively, both with the Army's 3rd Infantry, 2nd Brigade, have met in the desert, a world away from the Hudson Valley. They haven't heard from their sons in more than a month.

Both Seans graduated Cornwall High School – two years apart. They might have known each other for a short time in high school. Even if they didn't, Jerry and Mary know each other from when they used to work together at St. Luke's Cornwall Hospital.

William Sean Kiernan's journey into military service seemed natural. Jerry met William Sean's mother, Vicki, in the U.S. Air Force. The two served in the Vietnam War. And even before that, William Sean's grandmother was an Army nurse captain during World War II. "This is just something you do," Jerry says. "You pay back what you need to, to this country, then you move on."

The last time Jerry and Vicki spoke with their son, he wanted them to send him snickers and a carton of Camel Lights cigarettes. "He thought he was going to quit because he wouldn't have access to them," Jerry says laughing. Dad sent some smoking cessation patches.

Sean Ward turned 20 on Feb. 12. He was somewhere in the Middle East for his birthday. "It's hard watching it on TV," Mary says of the war. "But at the same time it's compelling...........And you hope to catch a glimpse (of Sean)."

Mary says Sean didn't enlist in the Army right away. He spent a year at college, but after Sept. 11 he felt "compelled" to go. Sean's father was in the Marine Corps. And, Mary says, Sean was "born with a GI Joe in his hands."

She doesn't know where Sean is exactly. But his unit follows the 7th Cavalry into combat. Sean's unit is called the "tip of the spear". So chances are he's somewhere in the desert of Iraq by now.

So as the war wages on, this father in Cornwall and this mother in Durham, N.C., stay in contact via e-mail and by phone. The waiting is hard to do alone.

The process of setting up and completing the interview was a good diversion for the Kiernan's and us. It gave us an opportunity to speak warmly about our sons. We both knew this newspaper interview would a good vehicle to get the message out to their friends from high school that their buddies were in the war.

The first week of the war we connected with friends and family all over the United States. Our phone was ringing non-stop the entire first weekend. Former co-workers from New

York, friends from high school to graduate school called or emailed, there was an amazing outpouring from both people currently in our lives and people we hadn't heard from in years. Everyone asked for his address. Most of our family and friends sent him packages and letters. Sean has since reported to me that the most useful packages were from Tom and Tom's brother, Chris Ward. They always included little things like nail clippers and duct tape.

My sister, Jessica, called me every single day to check in and see how I was. Jess was incredible. Through her organizational efforts nearly everyone who worked with her sent Sean packages. Of course we had no idea he wouldn't get them until mid-April. The soldiers on the front line were not receiving mail for weeks at a time. Sean reports that by the time he finally got his mail there were so many backlogged boxes that he got tons of them at once. Jessica's co-workers continued their efforts until he came home.

A powerful day for us was when the 507th Maintenance Company had been attacked. We understood from news reports American soldiers were killed and some were taken as prisoners. The hard reality of war set in. It would be hours before any of the families of the soldiers would be notified. Our thoughts were not of our son Sean but of Jerry and Vicki's son, W. Sean. We knew he was a mechanic in a Transportation Company but we didn't know the identity of the company. A mutual friend from Cornwall, Mary Ellen Albarino, called to let us know she was with the Kiernan's and would stay with them until they could confirm whether or not W. Sean was in the 507th. We agonized with them and realized, at that moment, how physically alone we were in Durham.

It was important to us to feel touched by friends. Whether they were long distance, long time friends or new friends, we both felt comforted when people reached out to us. One day at work I was watching CNN on the TV across the hall from my office and saw that a 3rd ID soldier had been killed. I don't know why it struck me hard that day but it did. I broke out in a sweat. I felt trapped at work. An acquaintance at Duke reached out to me and offered to go to lunch with me. We went to Duke Gardens and enjoyed the peaceful beauty. It was a godsend. I had felt like I was going to hyperventilate and was rescued just in time.

The phone was a lifeline. I was surprised when my best friend from childhood, Anne Principe, called. We email each other frequently but I hadn't spoken to her in years and yet she cared enough to pick up the phone and call me. My good friend, Debbie De Jesus, called me almost daily. I would bring my cell phone to work and call her while I walked the half-mile to my car every day after work. She was always there for me just like my sister. Debbie is in New York and my sister is in San Francisco, yet somehow between the two of them, they kept my spirit together and never let me down. They both care about Sean nearly as much as I do. It is the history I have shared with them that helped me through this. They know a lot about Sean and a lot about me. They let me be who I am and I love that. They both can make me laugh in an instant even when I'm in a sour mood! Even more importantly they wrote to Sean and let him know how much they cared about him.

We were also in contact with Erik's family. The 82nd Airborne had left in the beginning of March. The news was dominated by the efforts of the Marines and the 3rd ID. We were hearing very little about the 82nd so we touched base with them for any news they may have received. Erik's mom, Debbie, shared that she was having difficulty sleeping; unfortunately, I knew exactly what she was talking about.

At work I attempted to concentrate. I checked the Fox homepage on the Internet often. Sometimes I caught a clip of Greg Kelly who was embedded with the 3rd ID. David Bloom's report would sometimes be available on MSNBC's website and I would check that out too. By 4 p.m. in the afternoon I was spent and would go home. I considered taking a leave of absence but thought better of it since that would be a financial hardship. Most of the time, work was a good place to be, it was a necessary distraction. Yet, the graduate course I was taking was proving to be a challenge I hadn't expected. I was exhausted at the end of the workday and the last thing I wanted to do was coursework. I decided the only way to cope was to take a day off now and then to catch my breath.

A week or so into the war I took a "catch my breath" day. Tom and I took a ride to Fayetteville. He wanted to shop for a new gun at a pawnshop just outside of Ft. Bragg. It was a place Sean had brought him when he was home in December.

At the pawnshop, Tom found the pistol he was looking for and headed to the counter to pay for it. As he was walking to the cashier he was distracted by the footage of the war that was on about ten televisions that line the shelf near the entrance. Rather than go to the cashier he walked over to where the TV's were to get a better view of the firefight. It was the 3rd ID 2nd Brigade and the machine gunners were prominent. We, of course, couldn't tell if it was Sean but the combat we were watching raised the hair on the back of our neck. However, no one was as interested in the scene as much as we were and certainly not the store manager. The poor guy thought Tom was trying to leave the store without paying for the gun. It took some explaining on our part but in the end every one calmed down. It didn't turn out to be a relaxing day. I began to understand that no matter what I did or where I was I wouldn't be able to relax until I knew Sean was safe.

Amazingly a few days after Sean's first letter we received another one. Only this one wasn't in an airmail envelope and it didn't say "free mail" where the postage is normally located. Instead it was in a white envelope with a stamp and was postmarked March 28th. We got the letter on March 31st. Since it wasn't through the normal channel I was terrified to open it.

Hey Whats Up!
3/24/04
   I'm glad to be able to write to you. I'm in a 6' x
6' pit in the middle of Iraq south of the Euphrates

River. Its getting very dark. Not much time to write. NBC Anchor Brian Williams is going to drop this off when he gets back to the states. Its insanely intense. And a one of a kind experience. All I can say right now is that 2 days ago I earned my CIB. That's a good story.

I can't wait to see you guys and come back alive. Oh I forgot, we are guarding a Chinook that got hit w/an RPG7 and is down. We are going to be here a while till its taken away. I took as many photos as I can of everything w/out giving up our position.

Now I can't see a damn thing so I have to stop cause we have noise and light discipline in effect.

See you in the States,
Sean

Tom and I had watched this story on the NBC Evening News with Tom Brokaw. Tom wondered out loud at the time if Sean's unit was involved. We wondered that a lot during this period. We were never really sure about anything including where Sean was.

After reading the letter I tracked down Brian William's office to thank them for getting the letter to us so quickly. I was sure they had no idea what it meant to us. It wasn't easy to locate someone on his staff that I could speak to without getting put into voicemail. I persevered and finally reached his assistant. She had been the one to put the stamps on the letters and get them out in the mail.

I explained to her that we had not heard from him since the beginning of the war and that although we had received a letter prior to this one it had been written before the start of the war. I told her that to have confirmation that he was doing okay was just incredible. I think she felt as good as I did.

The letter Sean wrote on 3/24/03 confirmed to Tom and I that we have a sixth sense about our children's well being. On March 22, 2003 at approximately 1:00 p.m. Tom sensed Sean was in danger. He became obsessed thinking about Sean and his whereabouts. Obviously Tom knew Sean was in a dangerous environment all the time at that point but this felt different to him. Tom tried to convey the feelings he was having about Sean, only he couldn't find the words to describe it. He felt Sean was involved in the battle that was televised on Saturday.

The letter we received on 3/24 tells us more than that he was guarding the downed helicopter. He tells us that two days prior to this incident he earned his combat infantryman badge; that would put the date of that engagement on 3/22/03, the day Tom felt apprehensive. Most importantly it tells us he was in a fire-fight that day being shot at and firing his weapon on the enemy. It was a significant day for him and us.

Tom was sensing that his son was in physical danger. The kind of danger a father tries to prevent from happening to his son. He yearned to be there fighting alongside Sean and to pro-tect him when necessary. He felt it intensely on March 22 and Sean's letter provided the proof that he indeed did have a sixth sense that day.

The next letter we received from Sean confirms the sixth sense I experienced. Typically I run on the treadmill before work each morning. During the war I tried not to miss a day. I needed to be sure I was holding the stress levels down and run-ning usually helped. As the 3rd ID moved closer to Baghdad I worried constantly about chemical weapons being used by the Iraqi's. I was also hearing that the troops were not getting sup-plies, and that food was limited to one MRE a day. The troops were sleeping in holes that they dug in the ground called hasties. The embedded reporters were doing a good job of showing us just how dirty, tired and courageous the troops were.

When I got up in the morning I would have my coffee, catch up on emails and the morning news. Typically Tom was getting up at 4 a.m. during this period and could fill me in on any important conflicts I may have missed during the night. Once I had my morning catch up I would get on the treadmill out in the garage. To get through the tedium of running in place I cranked the music up. The combination of the music, the exercise and the recent news reports would serve to send my emotions spiraling. I often found myself choking back the tears; if you've ever tried to run while crying you'll understand why I tried not to let the tears loose.

On the morning of April 1st I couldn't hold a single positive thought in my mind. The media was focused on how and when we would take Baghdad. The whole idea of taking Baghdad, in my mind, meant several outcomes were possible: we would take the city without much of a struggle, we would be engaged in urban warfare or the Iraqis would launch chemical weapons and destroy us. It was difficult to stay positive. My heart was heavy all day.

I have a friend, Carol Hayter Bomba, who is my best email buddy. I met Carol in the on-line MPA program and we found we had a lot in common. For the first semester and a half we did not meet face to face yet somehow we realized in our emails that we had a special bond. Our email correspondence began in September 2001 and has continued through today.

Sometimes I wish I had kept all of our emails. They are a great collection of our thoughts and life's ups and downs. Over the past few years we shared so much: the MPA program; rigorous courses and papers; the wedding of Carol's daughter, Allysha; the birth of her grandchildren; and the Empty Nest Experience, my two children left for college and the military and her newly married daughter moved thousands of miles away to Hawaii. What one of us didn't understand the other did. During our MPA program, Carol was the one who taught me not to hit the send button when I was ready to shoot off an email giving the professor a lashing about the workload that had been assigned. I was fiery and Carol was controlled. We've also shared the disability of our husbands and all that goes with it. We found a sisterhood in this aspect of our lives. We learned from each other that we were more than survivors we were thrivers. Then there was the war and all that it brought with it. My concentration was poor and I was struggling with the MPA course. Carol carried me through the last leg of the graduate journey. She kept me going when I was ready to quit. She talked me into sending her my drafts. Just when I thought I had enough she would make me laugh and remind me that we had to finish together.

During the three weeks of war Carol added a new dimension to our email friendship by writing a prayer for me every day. Unbeknownst to me she kept a copy of all of the prayers, put them in a special book and sent it to me once Sean was safely home. She encouraged me to write them too but I didn't have the heart for it. Prayer was a constant source of comfort for me; however, to speak the words of my prayers was too much for me to bear. I couldn't bring myself to find the words until April 1st.

I was having that feeling that I get when something troubling is happening with one of my children. I couldn't tell anyone exactly what it was but it was a sense of dread that things weren't right. My heart was exploding so I wrote this prayer in an email to Carol:

> *A Mother's Prayer.........*
> *Dear Jesus,*
>
> *Be with my Sean tonight. Sit on his shoulder and tell him to do what he knows is right and he will be safe.*
>
> *Urge him to follow his instincts, his first instincts, and to stick with it.*
>
> *Remind him that when he changes the first answer on a test it ends up being wrong..........He mustn't second guess himself tonight.*
>
> *He is deep in battle tonight. Lord, bring the Angels with you and surround him. Protect him and his fellow soldiers.*
>
> *Please hug him for us and give him strength tonight.*
>
> *April 1, 2003*

This prayer would not become significant until I found out

that Sean wrote us a letter that same day expressing his mental and physical state. I didn't receive the April 1st letter from him until the end of April so I didn't put this together with what I was feeling that day until Carol sent the pray book and realized the power of the "sixth sense".

The sixth sense I have as a mother revolves around my children's emotional and spiritual health. My heart broke when I read the last letter he wrote while still in combat:

April 1, 2003
Mid Afternoon

How's everything back home? Is it still cold? Its hot as hell over here and cold as the Artic at night. My hair is as long as can be, and I think I'm thinner than I was straight out of Basic Training.

Mail goes out every day now, we found out today. If I get more opportunities I'm going to write. I can't talk about the future, only whats happened and whats been done. I'm not going to talk about my experiences in combat those are best left for a barbecue and a few brews. I can tell you that the worst is yet to come. Where we are going some people might not return. So far Task Force 1-64 hasn't lost anyone. We were fortunate. I can't say its going to be alright. That's a lie. I can tell you that from the Intel we have and the experiences I have, that Haji sucks. He sucks bad. I am truly confident in myself, my equipment, my brothers, and my weapon. No Fear.

I don't think I'm going to be home anytime soon. The one thing about war is that when the pace is fast, time flies. Down time is welcomed, and you never want it to end. Tomorrow it ends.

Positive thoughts are not hard to come by. Its not like me to ponder about my demise. That for the most part is out of my control. No sense in even

worry or thinking bout it. Days like today and yes-
terday I sit in my 6' x 3' hole and think about my
car, you guys, homemade cakes, Jen.

I'm hungry, very hungry. MRE's are meant to
sustain you w/just enough calories to keep you
going, not to fill you up. Not a bad thing, just some-
thing you not used to you know? We have not been
able to receive mail since we've been out here. That
sux. You really look forward to gettin mail.

Hey you know what I can't wait to get back into,
is the shower you have in the master bedroom, and
the Jacuzzi I've never used.

So How's work Ma? How's painting Dad? Any
new research developments? Any new rifles? How's
Kate doing? Whats she up to? How's the dog?
How's the rest of the family?

If you think about it there's really nothing left
for me in the Army. I've earned my CIB witch is the
soul reason you join the Infantry. Actually I'm going
to go for the EIB and then that's it. Then when we
get back and after I have that I might as well
change my MOS or go Green to Gold or something.

I'm going to close it up for now. Go write a let-
ter to Jen now. She's out here too, somewhere.
Should drop her a line too. If Erik's out here he
probably got his CIB too. I know that the 82 seized
Baghdad International Airport. So I'm sure he's
seen something. Gotta go right now so I'll see you
when I see you.

Love,
Sean

How does it feel to have your child's life in danger 24 hours
a day, 7 days a week? I'm not sure that there are words to
describe the intensity of emotions. I was incredibly proud of
him and the dedication he showed toward his citizenship as well

Sean took this photograph of himself a few days before the invasion of Baghdad right around the time he wrote the April 1 letter.

as his remarkable integrity to follow his heart and soul. Yet, there were times I was intensely frightened for him. I did manage to find an inner strength through prayer that helped me quiet my rising fears. I worked at not being fearful for his life and concentrated instead on how well he was trained to complete the mission. I knew he was where he wanted to be and needed to be. He wouldn't have it any other way.

Ultimately as parents we are never ready for our children to die. Nor are we ever ready to send them to fight in a war where the possibility of their deaths is in our thoughts. Nothing can prepare us for this death, so we go on and pray for strength should that unfortunate day arrive.

The war was terribly difficult for families of soldiers but then again the occupation after the war officially ended has been as well, maybe more so. The after combat turmoil has been dangerous, deadly and unnerving. After the embedded reporters left their units the news began to dry up. It was challenging to find out information about the 3rd ID. This was particularly distressing as we began to wait for word of the 3rd ID's redeployment date. Our new mission was to look forward to the much-anticipated homecoming. There were times when it felt like it was never going to happen.

Sean had written one other letter before the war began; however, we didn't receive it until the middle of May. This was upsetting because he had asked for some much needed supplies. When we realized that the letter was written on March 16th (it was postmarked on April 29th) we knew he had gone through the war not having these items and we hoped he realized that the only reason he didn't get them was because we hadn't received his letter.

> *03/16/03 Sunday*
>
> *I'm only going to write a quick letter, if that's possible. I got to go to Mass for the second time since I've been here, the first was for Ash Wednesday. It was outside this time, and it was surrounded by photographers, a little distracting it was. Its nice to go to Mass every now and then. Its like a 1 hour vacation. It hits the spot.*
>
> *My squad leader, Sgt. Hernandez, takes lots of digital photos of us. He sent the one I'm sending you home to be printed on photo quality paper. It came out pretty good. It's the only one I got right now. I figured there's no reason for me to have it, considering how I live w/these people. It's a picture of the whole platoon. Guys in my squad are Sgt. Hernandez, Cp. Wysocki, Sgt. Teodoro, Spec Mantle, PFC Ward, PFC Munoz, PFC Vanderlinde, PV2 Smith, PV2 Burress. In order from highest rank to lowest. The other PFC's have been out there longer except, my date of rank is before Aug. 02 so I rank them all. Pretty cool. It pays to be intelligent.*
>
> *Two days ago our company and Task Force reaffirmed our Patriotic oath. It was pretty cool, except we had to stand at attention in "full battle rattle" and that kind of took away from the whole moment.*
>
> *But on another note, if you could send some things that are now impossible to get over here, that*

would be great. Ok, I need D size batteries, at least three AA batteries, duck tape blk or green, 550 cord, and something to clean the lens on my scope. O, another toothbrush, and the most important item is the best electric razor money can buy. Use my money if you have to. Send some of the photos of the family if you can spare them. The house and the car would make good photos too. Just have someone take photo's of you guys, bring them to 1 hour photo, drop them over to me.

Its funny how you see who your true friends are when you deploy. The fact is, the only friends I got are my brothers and sisters in the Army, and my family. Its pretty messed up when you live in a life or death situation every day and they can't take the ten seconds to write me one sentence.

Well, in all actuality I'm glad they don't write. This way we can cut the bullshit and stop wasting everybody's time. Ok, now that I've got that off my chest!:) I can move on.

My one best friend here is Munoz. He's real cool, and we have similar interests. The other is Mantle. Sgt. Hernandez says we are exactly alike. Good stuff.

Well its 1532 and I'm gonna go get some shut eye cause I got the 4 – 5 shift tomorrow morning. Gotta be alert when its for real. So I hope you guys enjoy the photo, sorry, I don't have more. Tell Kate I said hi. I sent her an 11 page letter yesterday, finally.

Ok, I really gotta go eat some lovely chow, and my pen just broke. Love you guys, keep me in mind.

Love,
Sean

We set about getting all of the supplies that he had request-ed hoping they would still be useful for him. I asked the staff at the Duke Eye Center Optical Shop if they had glass cleaner for his scope. Before I knew it they had given me boxes of sunglasses, cleaners and cloths to wipe the lens with. Sean reports that as soon as he opened the box of sunglasses the troops wiped him out. Apparently sunglasses were a hot commodity by then.

As great as the letters were we were anxious to speak with him and to hear the sound of his voice. The day before Mother's Day I encouraged Tom to go to a life drawing class. He didn't like leaving the house out of concern that he would miss a phone call from Sean. Jerry and Vicki's son, W. Sean, had called them by then. We suspected he would be calling soon. We also realized he may not be in an area where phones were readily available. We were anxious to hear how he was handling the experience he had just been through.

In any event I convinced Tom to go and get away from the house for a few hours. I was planning on touching up my final paper and then going for a good long run. As I sat down to write the phone rang. I picked it up and there was a delay. I remembered from Sean's earlier calls from Camp New York that there was a delay when we spoke. It was maybe ten seconds from the time he spoke to the time I heard him. So I stayed on the line until I heard a voice. When his voice finally reached me I was overjoyed!

I could hardly contain myself. He sounded wonderful. The phone delay makes a conversation difficult. We end up talking over one another so to avoid the problem I stopped talking and listened to him. He was at the Al Rasheed Hotel in Baghdad. Sean said they were at the hotel because they had taken it over a few days after they fought their way into Baghdad. He said there was sporadic water and electricity. He had taken one shower and was sleeping in a bed; however, he said the bedding was as dirty as the floor.

Sean was as delighted to hear my voice, as I was his. He filled me in on where he had been and what he was currently doing. I could hear his disappointment when I told him his dad wasn't home. He told me he heard they would be home by the end of

June and couldn't wait for that day to arrive.

We had a family reunion planned for the end of July and he felt sure he would be home for it. We were going to a beautiful Lake George resort with my extended family. He would get to relax and hang around with his sister and cousins for a week. We've been there before so he knew full well the fun that awaited him. He was really looking forward to it.

I realized Sean didn't know the next day was Mother's Day and yet his call was a gift. The burden of worry had been lifted just a little and I wanted to share that with Tom. To capture the essence of the call I wrote Tom the following note:

> *Dear Tom,*
>
> *A Mother's Day gift arrived for me today. It was a once in a lifetime gift, literally. It was delivered like this:*
>
> *Ring, ring, ring....I pick up the phone, there is a delay and I think "AT&T again, do they ever give up??" As is our custom I wait to hear who it is just in case....and a voice says "Ma, its Sean, do you know where I am?" My internal thoughts are to be calm and listen.*
>
> *He says "Hey I'm in the Al Rasheed hotel. Some guy is putting in Verizon phones and I asked to borrow his cell phone to call you, and he let me so I only have about 10 minutes. There is a 10 second delay on the phone."*
>
> *AND he sounds absolutely wonderful. He doesn't like it and he likes it. How Sean, huh? He has no idea who Ron Martz is and thinks maybe it is a different Charlie Company. He is getting packages every day but really looks forward to letters. He thinks maybe the end of June they will be coming home but it changes all the time. He wrote to Jen and invited her to The Sagamore. He wrote us letters and sent a map.*

He wrote of a battle in pieces, so it will come in different letters, he doesn't mind talking about it, it just takes a long time to write his thoughts out and he gets tired. He writes of this battle because he may be awarded a BRONZE STAR.

He has been given leadership of his squad. He likes the leadership role. He can't wait to come home.

He sounds wonderful, did I say that already? Wanted to know where you were. Couldn't believe you weren't home and he thought Kate would have been here too. He has showered in the hotel, has bed bug bites and his uniform is grossly dirty. He doesn't particularly like getting candy, says it will make him gain weight but looks forward to getting the stuff you sent him last week.

Ten minutes goes by quickly with the delay as you have to be so disciplined when talking to him not to override him but not let him hang either.

Now that there are phones in the hotel getting hooked up maybe he will call more often as he only has tons of calling cards to use.

His manner is that of our Sean, sure and confident and knowing that he will come home to us and be cared for by us.

I'm off to get my massage but I wanted you to know all of this.

Love,
Me

After I wrote this for Tom, I called our families. They were nearly as excited as I was. The entire family was anxious to hear from him. It seemed to end the sense of dread the war created for us. Now we could begin to concentrate on his homecoming.

As upset as Tom was that he missed Sean's call, he was thrilled that I was there. His concern all along has been that one of us be available to talk to Sean when he called. Because of that concern we adopted the habit of call-forwarding our home phone to our cell phone.

We received occasional phone calls after this first one. It was difficult for Sean to find the time or the availability of a phone. Because we were able to call forward I don't believe we missed one call. In one of his letters he describes his frustration with the phones not always working and one time forgetting our phone number. Losing track of one another was one of my earlier concerns when we first moved to Durham.

The month of May had many ups and downs for all of us. With the reporters no longer embedded with the troops we weren't receiving the same quantity and quality of information we had relied on in the past. We scanned the Internet on a regular basis for any news regarding the 3rd ID and relied on whatever information Sean relayed through phone calls and letters.

Our experience as the parents of a single (unmarried) soldier was not unusual. Most of the parents do not live near their daughter or son's base and are out of the social and information loop; whereas spouses of soldiers often live on or near the base having greater access to information and to each other. Typically these soldiers are the youngest in the unit having left the home they were raised in to join the Army. More attention is paid to the families (wives and children) of the married soldiers, and rightly so, however, most of the single troops also belong to a family that loves them, misses them, worries about them and has a vested interest in knowing where they are and when they would be redeployed (returning to their home base).

They were ready to come home and the families were ready to have them home. Most of the 3rd ID had been there since September 2002. The media was reporting various dates the 3rd ID would redeploy. It was frustrating when those dates would arrive without redeployment on the horizon.

During this period of time we had other family details that needed attention. We picked Kate up from Endicott College in Beverly Massachusetts. It was not an easy good-bye for her since she made the decision to be closer to us and transfer to a

University North Carolina, about 2 hours from Durham. Knowing she wasn't coming back was difficult for her.

Kate had great roommates. They all took good care of one another. They were particularly adept at helping her overcome waves of homesickness. The day they said goodbye was emotional, they all wept together in a big hug.

Kate had enjoyed living in close proximity to Boston and her good friend, Caitlin Delaney, from high school. Caitlin was attending school south of Boston while Kate was north of the city. A few times they took the train to see one another. This was one of the things that Kate would miss when she transferred.

On the way back from moving her out of her dorm we stopped to see Tom's parents in Connecticut and then our friends in Cornwall. I was graduating from Marist College that week as well. Marist is just 45 minutes from Cornwall. Our friends in Cornwall were kind enough to invite us to stay with them for a few days. It was a comforting feeling to be with people we had known for years, we could relax in a way we hadn't been able to since we moved to Durham.

Graduation was a spectacular event. The program I had completed was the first on-line master of public administration programs in New York State. Most of the professors and the students had not yet met face to face. It was fun to finally see what each other looked like. The college held a dinner for us the night before graduation to honor our dedication and motivation. There were approximately 30 students that started with our cohort group and just 13 that went the distance. Our on-line discussions are now used as part of the courses for some of the professors. I was thrilled that I had not dropped the last course, as I would have missed the wonderful celebrations as well as the opportunity to finally meet each of the cohorts.

To add to the fun of graduating I found out Vicki Kiernan was graduating the same day. She had completed her bachelor's degree and would be there as well. We had commiserated so much over our son's welfare while serving in Iraq that it was terrific to have the opportunity to finally have a reason to rejoice.

*The day Vicki and I graduated from Marist College with the 3rd
Infantry Division patch on our graduation caps.*

She created a large 3rd ID patch that we put on the top of our
mortarboards. In a sea of hats we were the only two with the
patches; it demonstrated our solidarity. It seemed fitting that
the day of graduation was also Armed Forces Day. We each sent
pictures to our sons. Sean thought it was pretty cool.

The visit north was a good diversion for us. In retrospect, the
rest of the month seemed to be a constant conversation about
Sean, the 3rd ID, and their return home. On returning home
from work each day I was to find Tom in the garage painting or
reading. We both anticipated the mail like we were waiting for
the million-dollar check. We watched the news constantly and
Tom scoured the Internet for any bit of news about the 3rd ID.

It must have been excruciating for Kate. Here she was home
from her first year of college, with no job and no friends. She

had no one to go out with to get away from us and all we did was talk about Sean. Little did she realize how she held me up during this time; she is a joy to have as a daughter. She lights up every room she enters. When I came home from work she was there to help with dinner and spice things up with different meals. Nearly every evening we went for a walk. On those walks we would have many deep conversations; it was an opportunity for both of us to share our thoughts with one another. Since the walks were relatively short we often continued our talks when we kayaked on the weekends.

We kayaked just about every Sunday afternoon. We were so silly on the darn thing. We would take it out in the middle of the lake and just laze around waiting for the motorboats to throw us a wake we could ride on. We rarely worked hard paddling and when we did we would bust out laughing at ourselves. We took pictures of ourselves and sent them to Sean.

I'll never forget when she said to me on one of those kayaking days, "Mom, I feel insignificant compared to Sean and what he is doing." All I could say to her was that I did too. As it turns out Tom was also feeling this way. We all did. She worried about him, loved him and couldn't stand hearing anymore about his situation, which brought its own level of frustration. Being a sister myself I understood completely. My oldest brother has achieved more financially than I could ever hope to. He gives my parents expensive gifts, takes his extended family on vacation and doesn't have to worry about his finances. There was a time I couldn't stand hearing anymore about his achievement from my parents so in a way I understood Kate's feelings. Yet it was different for Kate because it was compounded by the fact that her brother was still in constant danger. I give her credit for expressing her feelings and relieving herself of the burden by sharing it.

To help her overcome these frustrations Kate wrote him letters and baked him spectacular cookies. Sean called her after he got them to tell her they were bakery quality. In fact he reported that the package had been damaged and there was sand stuck to the jelly cookies. Even the sand couldn't keep him from enjoying the cookies down to the last crumb.

One of Kate's summer projects was to paint both hers and Sean's bedrooms. Since she is an interior design student we left the choice of colors to her. She chose deep colors for her room and soothing ones for Sean's because we wanted him to have a relaxing, peaceful environment when he came home for visits. It was a great project for her to immerse herself in, using both her newfound skills and the need to do something for her brother.

Tom and I were concerned about Sean's emotional health. Through our phone communications with Sean he didn't express that he was having a difficult emotional time but we were also aware that he might experience posttraumatic stress symptoms once he returned to the states. We decided to educate ourselves about its signs and symptoms. Tom's research turned up a few good books that were useful in this regard. One piece of valuable information discussed the importance of the combat veteran's ability to talk about his experience. Talking about the experience becomes a way of cleansing the spirit for the warrior. We encouraged Sean to express his experiences in writing either in a confidential journal or in letters home and write he did:

> *May 03*
> *Page 1*
>
> *I remember it like it was yesterday. In fact whenever I get five minutes to think of something I'm either replaying what happened a thousand times over or thinking about sex. So you could imagine that I do a lot of thinking. In all honesty what happened to me and my team on the fourth of April will change a man. It will make all of us appreciate the value of life that much more.*
>
> *It was very hot, already. It was very early in the morning but the back of the Bradley gets hot enough to be a Jenny Craig Sauna. It gets the worst around noon time, its hardly bearable, its hard to believe that human life can be sustained in the back*

*of a Brad. It just doesn't seem there's enough oxy-
gen go to around. Especially when they are over-
crowded. We had people sitting on the floor b/c we
ran out of seats. Terrible. A thing a man tries very
hard to forget. The best and only way to cope w/it is
to fall asleep. Some people like to call it falling
asleep, I like to call it waiting to pass out. You pray
for that coma to come, and if it doesn't, well its kind
of like harassing a badger in a cage until the point
where it nearly kills itself trying to escape.*

*So there I was trying to sleep, with my ear plugs
in and my Kevlar off and my body armor open, trying not to overheat. The only thing I remember is
being woken up, so I guess I passed out, and being
told to get ready to dismount. I got my gear on
miraculously in the tight confines of the land sub-
marine, waited for the metallic, hydraulic click and
hum of the ramp dropping. I ran out the back of the
Brad w/ a purpose, the last man out behind the
grenadier who carries an M203 40mm grenade
launcher. So it was me, Sgt. Teodoro my team
leader, Pvt. Burress, and Spc. Mantle had to ride
on a different track due to space and mission prior-
ities. So to say the least we were undermanned, No
biggie, in our track rides a M240B gun team, so we
definitely had firepower. The rest of the squad had
to be in a different location, leaving us separated
from the squad and the platoon.*

*When you are in the back of a Brad its difficult
to know your surroundings when all you have is several periscopes to view through. You have to rely on
quick thinking, you have to perceive, recognize and
identify, those are things that would help me later
on that day and the following days 3 key elements
that led to my safety and survival. When Bravo
team, my team, dismounted it was the first real*

good look we had at our surroundings, and the first time I stepped on the streets of Baghdad. I was told to take up a position behind a guard rail overlooking what looks like a park in a city, a small park with many trees along the outskirts. Burress was to my left and Sgt. Teodoro to his left. We awaited for further orders.

Within seconds the orders come to cross the street and take up positions. I was placed alongside a palm tree w/tall grasses growing close to its base. Burress was 5m to my right and Sgt. Teodoro on the left side, opposite side, of the tree I was at. We pulled security and waited for the 240 gun team to set up tripod and get their visual sectors laid out to them as well. A few quick minutes later they were ready to go. Sgt told Buress to run get his E-tool. It was at this time that I was told to start digging while Burress remained in the prone pullin security.

It was at this time that I found out our Bradley was not going to be along side us. We also knew what our objective was by this time. Our mission was to protect the East flank of White Platoon's M1A1 Abrams tanks. So we were not left totally in the dark.

As I began to dig you can, or rather I did look around. Off to my right across the highway was the Tomb of the Unknown Soldier. It was absolutely enormous. Behind our position approximately 800 meters out is one of the Iraqi Ministry buildings, looks like twelve stories high. Way out in the distance, 360 degrees was huge clouds of smoke streaming from freshly pummeled enemy occupied buildings.

I brought my E-tool up over my head and swung in a violent downward motion to start my hasty fighting position. This is a process that does not nor-

mally take more than 30 minutes. In this case it took hours. Off our right incoming mortars were impacting no more than 200 – 250 meters away. Each time a round would come in we would bury our faces in the soft black dirt of the park and hope that no shrapnel would come our way. That kind of stuff didn't bother me, and I didn't feel really threatened by it. Mortars from Iraqi's is not the most disturbing thing they can throw at you. RPG's is another thing. Iraqi's have RPG's like American families have dogs. No family is complete w/o one.

Its not something that right away you think to yourself o shit I'm being shot at. Its not something your use too, its not something you can practice. You can't realistically have a sniper shoot at you in training, so when it actually happens, its not freezing up, its more like your trapped in your own awe. Then it hits you. Those are rounds hitting the tree's 3 ft to my right. That's a bullet that just hit the guard rail that runs parallel to the road just behind me. The tank to my rear is being plinked by a guy w/ an AK-47. You could tell it was no trained sniper like U.S. Forces would have b/c n one in particular was focused on. It seemed like he just wanted to take his chances and launch a few rounds at the American forces before he got annihilated. When you can't tell where your taking fire from the only thing you can do is get down and fight the urge to look up or try to look and see where its coming from. All through out the first two days I was hunkered down in my hasty taking indirect fire of all sorts from mortars, to snipers, to RPG's, even sneak attacks by the Republican Guard, I should say attempted sneak attacks.

What I'm going to try to do is write to you in detail about my engagements that I incurred dur-

*ing my first few days in Baghdad. I'm going to send
these first four pages off to you, as it took me 3 days
to get the time to gather these thoughts together
and relive the moments minute by minute. I just
figured it would be interesting to know what I was
thinking about, and what my emotions were at the
time I was engaging the enemy. I can't describe it
well enough. I feel I want you to be in my head at
the moment you are reading this. I want you to feel
what it felt like. Pulling 100% security for 72
hours w/one meal a day. How strung out and
fatigued you get. It changes you. I'm going to call
these first four pages the prelude. This doesn't even
get started into the thick of it. Since I'm running
out of paper, I'll tell you that me and Burress are
being put in for ARCOM's with a V device. I don't
know if it will go through or not but its cool to
know. I think of you guys a lot.*

  Love,
  Sean

About two weeks later we received this letter:

*May 2003
Sunday 11:43*
  *I can't remember exactly where I left off. I do
remember that in my mind I left off as I was digging. It was while I was digging my hasty fighting
position that we made first contact. It was also me
who spotted first contact, my 20/15 vision comes in
handy.*
  *As I swung my E-tool upward I had happened
to look up, before I could finish my downward swing
I spotted someone peek out from behind the wall
that was 75-85 yards away. I instantly stopped, got
down into the prone and grabbed my M249 SAW,*

*while at the same time screaming "contact front!!!"
at the top of my lungs. All I knew was that we were
also located next to the tomb of the Unknown
Soldier in Baghdad. Therefore I was greatly aware
that civilians do live in this area, and I had to be
careful, and aware of my surroundings as well.*

*I remembered from a few weeks back when I
was on guard that we were told to yell "Imshee"
(that's not how you spell it, its how you say it
though) one time and if the intruder kept
approaching (Imshee means go away, or stay back
in Iraqi) to open fire on it. I was to yell it so loud
that it could wake every one up so they could
respond as well. We were never briefed on what to
do if we were to make contact, so I gave that contact
one chance, since I could see no substantial uniform
and my sixth sense said don't shoot.*

*I didn't shoot, nobody did. As I yelled Imshee,
about fifteen heads and torsos poked out from
behind crevices in the wall, and from behind the
gray, I forget the name, it looks like one of − a
gazebo, now I remember. Ok, yeah fifteen heads
popped out, and as I yelled in Iraqi, they scattered
like when you shoe flies that are swarming a dead
carcass. They booked it, and I mean I think they
could have had an Olympic record they ran so fast.
It was actually kind of comical. You see they never
saw us, because we were behind a small, very small,
just small enough (or big enough, depending on
whether you like your cup half full or half empty)
to conceal the other men from my team and the
weapons squad on the other side of the tree all lying
in the prone pulling security.*

*Its funny cause had I not got on my knees to
start digging when I did, I never would've spotted
the people. The way we were setup, the security ele-*

ments wouldn't have picked up the contact till it could've been too late. Just in the right place at the right time. To fix that, we moved a tank up a couple of feet, because the gunner on top of the M1A1 Abrams main battle tank, manning the 240C (same as what the foot has, but no flash suppressor, or butt stock, gets mounted on the gunners hatch and shoots via dual thumb triggers at the rear, on a swivel mount. I like the 240 Charlie!) and his TC (Tank Commander) can see better because of their elevated position on top of the track.

Once the men realized what they stumbled upon, I think, or we initially agreed that the civilians were trying to move using available cover to avoid certain blocking positions, just trying not to get shot. Our opinion would most certainly change about what our friends were doing over by the gazebo in the near future.

After contact was made, my team put out (team leader Sgt. Teodoro) that we were going to pull 100% security all day and night to insure no surprise attacks when our guard was down or most vulnerable to be exact. We were also told if it walked in our sectors it had a death wish, and was to be shot. No more warnings, none. No shout, no shot, just shoot, no problem. That what we do best. Unfortunately, our team can't shoot (I don't know why I keep leaving leader out of "team leader", but its supposed to be there ok?), ok, so our team "leader" can't see, so he can't shoot and he always, or almost always has a misfire after the first shoot – so I got no faith in his shooting ability. there's plenty in mine and Burress', we both shot expert, no need to worry there. From what I recall all engagements took place no further out than 100 meters, so it was cake.

No breakfast, no lunch, no water except for can-

teens (2), no Bradley. Plenty of heat, too many Goddamn flies. It was so God-damn hot, it was like wearing five layers of clothes and a feather down jacket for two-a-day football practice in August. I mean my entire uniform under all my Body Armor, knee-pads and everything was absolutely soaked. Soaked to the bone, you could have rung it out and got sweat to drip out. After several hours into the afternoon your uniform that's exposed and not covered up by all the bullshit starts to dry up. It leaves salt stains around your knees where the padding was. No it doesn't just smell like vinegar, at one point or another you just accept you smell that rank smell that you acquire from the countless moments you break out in sweats, and dry up again, its not the smell that gets you. It's the thirsty hungry horny what ever the fuck they are, flies that swarm you because they like the salt stains.

The flies aren't even the worst problem oooo – no its when dusk arrives that you think you are getting a reprieve from your daily harassment of incessant mother-fuckin flies, but nature always has that funny way of finding out that your getting comfortable and likes too change that. It gets quiet for a moment while the flies mysteriously disappear, its not until when your sitting there, starting to think they are gone when it gets worse. They're like the kamikaze pilots of old. You here this buzzing sound, that's like a Japanese zero in for the kill. Zzzzzzzzzzzzzzz - right smack dead into your ear lobe, just like into the wooden decks of an old world war II carrier flight deck. Mosquitoes. Their the worst creation. Evil. Vile, relentless sons of bitches. You figure if you kill one of them, that friends would say, fuck this shit and try to find a new target. Mosquitoes are by far worse than flies. I hate them. there's nothing you can do except apply hydro corotzone and place a hankercheif on your face so they don't devour your face in its entirety.

Lets see, I think right now its about 1630 – 1730, somewhere around that time at the OPLP. Its going to get dark soon. The tankers have spotted movement all day. Its not until we get the word from higher to go and check out whats in front of our position, that we moved. I forgot to mention, that earlier my team did clear a bunker. That was pretty cool, but unfortunately uneventful. PVT Burress, Sgt. Teodoro, Sgt. Ski went on a flanking maneuver off to the right of our positions, to scan the slim and sparse tree-line to our front. They found, or stumbled upon a sandbag bunker about 50 meters to our front. PVT Burress and Teodoro each approached or rather charged the bunker with M16's blasting away. While standing on top of the edge of the sandbags, evaluating whether its clear or not, Teodoro doesn't detect any resistance or bodies, so he gives the word to head back.

Sgt. Teodoro gives us a quick brief as to what he saw. They saw boxes of RPG's, RPG launchers, and "rocket-propelled grenade launcher" fuses. There was one misfired RPG still smoking on the ground, and several Bandoliers of ammunition and magazines filled to the top of the magazines with 7.62x39 full metal jacketed bullets, the round I know so well. Due to the fact we had to return to our hastys and we couldn't clear farther out, Sgt. Teodoro gave Burress the order to launch his M203 grenade launcher at the bunker to take it out and destroy munitions inside.

I like leaving cliff hangers for you guys. So I'm going to only write 4 pages at a time about my experiences. I know it's a tease!! Hopefully I'll finish my

story in person. I'll write soon. Love you guys.
    Sean

In one of the packages he received there was a magazine with a good map in it of Baghdad so to better illustrate the he battle had been writing about he included it in his next letter.

05/08/03
    Ok, here it is. This is an extremely good and accurate map of Baghdad. I can tell my story really good. The area I circled was our sector. The X our hastys, the arrow the direction of fire. I had no idea there was command headquarters right there, but it makes sense. We took sniper fire from our rear in the ministry building. I put an X in the blast.
    Right now as I write this I am looking at the Council of Ministers building, that is shot to hell, from the Rasheed hotel (circled). And yes there is a pool here, and not its not filled. I wish it was.
    Things are good here. I think my arms got attacked by chiggers. That's about it. My hair is way too long again. According to the latest scuttlebutt we'll be in Camp New York by 22 of 05. Two days ago a guy from MCI pulled up and wanted to put a cell tower on the Rasheed. I said you can't come through this blocking position unless I can make a phone call with your cell. He said ok, here. "OK, HERE". Unfortunately its been so long I forgot the phone number, so I let my buddy use it. A great opportunity missed. Needless to say I still didn't let him through. Ha Ha.
    OK gotta split. Hope you enjoy the map. It shows exactly where I am, and you can better picture my engagements now. When I get back I'll show you where I've been. Almost everywhere on the map, and I'll show you the places I had some

discreet pickup truck rides with Iraqi Commandos.
That's another beer story. Well I'm going to sleep,
cause I can hardly write. See you when I see you.
     Sean

While compiling Sean's letters for this book I realized that he wrote a series of letters within the first week to ten days of May. We received his letters so far apart that it didn't occur to us how closely he had written them. After the group of battle letters he wrote, he didn't write again until June. It wasn't until he came home that I understood that the time between the first week of May and the beginning of June was a difficult period for him. For weeks he battled a gastrointestinal virus and waves of homesickness.

By mid-May Sean was calling more than writing. His conversations revolved around when they would be coming home. It seemed to be a different time frame every time we spoke to him. The changes in redeployment dates were beginning to wear thin. Initially he thought the 3rd ID would be home by the first week of June. A few times he was sure about a date only to be crushed with disappointment when it was cancelled.

During this time he sent out a large number of postcards. In case he didn't have much time for writing, I sent him pre-addressed postcards for him to send back to me and other family members. He really liked that idea. He liked it so much that when he found postcards of the Al Rasheed hotel he sent those to people as well. He had no idea the joy he brought to those who received them. People from all over were calling to tell me they received a card from him. They simply loved it. They never expected him to write and definitely didn't expect a thank you from him. The packages and letters they sent him were an expression of their thanks for the work he was doing.

The following are two of the postcards Sean sent to us:

Hi Mom –
     I've gotten just about all the mail by now. I

appreciate all the things you send me. It is important that I hear from you, sometimes war can be lonely.
Everything is good here, hope it is there too!
The son,
Sean

• • •

Hi Dad –
I finally got the care packages, they are great and come in handy. I'm staying at the Al Rasheed Hotel and drinking Pepsi's. Not so bad. Hope to shoot my .45 soon. See you when I get there.
Love,
Champion

And one from the Al Rasheed:

Hi Mom, Dad & Kate!
This is just a quick note to tell you that I am going to be home before June 1 guaranteed to us by a 3 Star General. I should be back at camp NY by the 10th of May to make some phone calls. Talk to you guys very soon!

Two postcards to my sister Jess and her family:

Hi Aunt Jess, Uncle Kenny and the girls!
Everything is good here. I'm safe so that's good. I'm writing you from the Tomb of the Unknown soldier in the heart of Baghdad. I got these postcards from Mom so I could keep in touch quickly. Moms are so smart! Hope to see all of you at the Sagamore. That day can't come soon enough, trust me!
Love,
Sean

• • •

Whats up!

I hope everything is good there. It is here, so far. It looks like I'm going to be home before 1 June, so I can't complain. Tell the girls I thank them a thousand times over for the softball pictures and what they sent. It was great to hear from you guys, tell everybody I said hi!

Sean

The dates he talked about coming home didn't materialize. I don't know for sure since I wasn't actually with him but he must have been frustrated with the delays. I can hear in his letters and the postcards how he longed to come home and I could sense his disappointment when it didn't happen.

As we neared the end of May we began to think the 3rd ID wouldn't be home in early June. It just didn't seem possible with the unrest that was occurring in many areas of Iraq. If they sent the 3rd ID home they wouldn't have enough troops in country to do the necessary work. Sure enough, Sean called the first week of June to tell us they were moving out of Baghdad to Falluja. The troops that were in Falluja needed reinforcements. Until a sound troop rotation was in place the 3rd ID would stay in Iraq.

The move to Falluja would further delay his homecoming. Sean, Tom and I finally decided to plan on Sean being home by the middle of the fall. If it was earlier than that, great, if it was later then we would readjust as necessary.

At the same time the 3rd ID moved to Falluja Tom was experiencing new health-related issues. Tom's hands and lower arms had been causing him pain and he had been having constant fasciculation's (similar to twitching but more intense) in his muscles for the past few months. At one of his doctor appointments in May the doctor suggested he have a test for carpal tunnel syndrome. The test was done in June and the results were not encouraging.

I was not allowed in the room for this test. The technician

had told me that it was going to take a long time and that he would call me at my office when Tom was done. Because of Tom's cognitive disabilities I generally stay with him when he goes to medical appointments. Against my better judgment, I went back to my office to get some work done. When I didn't hear from the technician after an hour and a half I called to check on him. He told me that Tom had left at least a half an hour earlier. The area where the testing was done is a maze. Since he hadn't made it back to my office I was sure he was lost. I raced from my office to find him. I was angry with myself for leaving him there. In my heart I had known better than to do that. I walked all over the hospital looking for him. Finally, I went back to the clinic where I had originally left him and sure enough the tech was wrong. Tom was still there. In fact, he was still in the room being tested. I was fuming. To add to our misery the person doing the testing told him he should call his doctor to get the results in a few days, since it was more than a problem with his hands.

A few days later the doctor confirmed that it was not carpal tunnel but damage to various muscles in Tom's upper and lower body. It was a frightening time for us. We didn't understand what was happening to him. It is an awful experience to go in for a test thinking one thing and come out with something totally unexpected.

We were advised to make an appointment with a neurologist. However, the earliest appointment we could get was in September. We were going to have to go through the whole summer worrying about his health. No one should have to wait that long for a medical appointment particularly when there are worrisome symptoms. I asked Tom's primary care doctor to intervene on our behalf. She did and got us an appointment for mid-July.

In the meantime we did our own research of his symptoms on the Internet. Doing medical research on the Internet can be can be bad and good. For us, it was a little bit of both. We just couldn't get enough of the right information; this led to all kinds of unnecessary worry and confusion. Every time we put his symptoms into a Google search we came up with one diagnosis: Amyotrophic lateral sclerosis (ALS also known as Lou Gehrig's disease), a progressive neurodegenerative disease that is fatal. It was a terrible blow to think Tom may have this disease. On the other hand our Internet search led us to a wonderful medical center in Charlotte, The Carolina ALS/Neuromuscular Center. Eventually the Center would be instrumental in helping us understand what was wrong with Tom.

In July, before we found our way to the Center, we went to the local neurologist appointment Tom's primary care doctor had facilitated. He did his exam, asked us some questions, ordered some more tests and said he would see us in a few months. Before we could ask questions he told us he didn't know what Tom had and that it could be any one of a number of diseases. After that statement he walked out. We were dumbstruck. We didn't even get to ask him if he thought it was ALS, what he was ruling out and why he ordered those particular tests. At that point we began to think the worst and figured the doctor didn't want to confirm our fears until all the test results were back.

We had all the tests done and waited to get the results. But they didn't come. It was the first time one of Tom's physicians didn't send us a copy of the test results. In the past ten years we had received all of Tom's medical test results either by mail or phone. We are no strangers to the healthcare system yet we had never been through anything quite like this. All of his physicians in the past communicated well with us. Our suspicion that it was ALS was growing by leaps and bounds. Since we had little to go on we continued our Internet research. Not knowing what was wrong was quickly becoming a nightmare.

For Sean's safety we didn't discuss details about Tom's current health situation. Although we had a family policy to tell our children all we knew about Tom's condition right from the beginning of his illness, this time we held information back. We alluded to Tom's increasing weakness now and then so he wouldn't be completely surprised when he saw Tom again but didn't elaborate. Sean's job was to focus on his safety and those of his fellow soldiers, not worry about his family.

Through this period of time Tom never stopped his habit of searching the Internet every day for any news of the 3rd ID. Some of the best coverage was from Georgia's Atlanta Journal Constitution, other sources included, the New York and Washington D.C. papers. All of these papers were available on-line. On June 16th Tom discovered an article by Jonathon Foreman of The New York Post that disturbed us. The article was titled: Bring Home the 3rd ID. By the time I finished reading the article my blood was boiling.

Mr. Foreman writes:

> *The Pentagon's apparent desire to administer and pacify Iraq on the cheap isn't just risky policy, it's cruelly unfair to the troops on whom the burden is falling. It is especially unfair to the Third Infantry Division, which did a large part of the fighting in the war and has been serving under arduous conditions ever since.*
>
> *The 3ID's three brigades captured Baghdad at the end of the first week of April, and (until the last two weeks or so) have done the lion's share of securing and stabilizing the Iraqi capital. Indeed, both the Second and Third Brigades have all been in the Gulf for at least nine months (a long deployment for an army in which most personnel are married).*
>
> *They were due to go home at the end of May, to be relieved in place by fresh soldiers from the 1st Armored Division, and the 2d and 3d Armored Cavalry Regiments. (Other units that bore the brunt of the fighting have mostly gone home already.)*
>
> *But CENTCOM took massive media flak for the lack of security in Iraq's cities at the end of May,*

so the Army promised to increase the number of troops on the ground. It did so not by bringing in a fresh division, but by the quick fix of keeping the exhausted Third Infantry in and around Baghdad.

The 3ID does have considerable, immensely valuable experience of peacekeeping in Bosnia and Kosovo, whereas the 4th Infantry now deployed in Tikrit has none.

And many 3ID units, despite having borne the brunt of the war's combat operations, have acquitted themselves surprisingly well in Baghdad. (Unlike the Marines, who had to be pulled out after helping to take the Eastern part of the city, they were able to make the transition from killers to policemen very quickly).

But peacekeeping operations requires a patience that can't be expected of troops that have been worked into the ground. As one 2d brigade captain said to me even before the deployment was extended by another two months, "The men are simply spent."

The same is true of the divisions vehicles. Few tanks, Bradleys or humvees are now in condition to drive back to Kuwait, and many will have to be shipped back on flatbed trucks.

Yet the whole of the 2nd ("Spartan") Brigade, including the 4/64 armored battalion (in which I was embedded until recently) has now been ordered to Falluja, the No. 1 flashpoint in the country.

Leave aside the questionable logic of sending in a combat-weary tank unit – albeit one which has performed policing tasks magnificently – to perform tasks better suited to armored calvary and infantry. Why send worn-out soldiers – quite possibly at the end of their tether – to a matchbox like Falluja when there are thousands of fresh combat troops all over Iraq?

Not to mention the 1st Calvary Division, the 1st Infantry Division or the 25th Infantry Division, and significant parts of other units like the 82nd airborne – all or most of which are sitting pretty at home.

It may be that there are genuine strategic reasons for keeping these units in reserve, rather than rotating them through Iraq. There may also be a convincing argument even for using the battered 3ID to do the heavy lifting in places like Falluja, instead of relatively unblooded units like the 1st Armored.

But all of this seems to show that the U.S. Army should not be shrunk from 10 divisions to eight, as reportedly planned by Defense Secretary Donald Rumsfield. Indeed, given that its tasks now and in the future involve operations other than war, it may that our 10-division army is simply too small for the post 9-11 era.

As Lt. Col. Wesley of the 2nd Brigade Combat Team explains, when assessing the necessary size of the army "the real issue is the ability to sustain force projection over time." (For every division on deployment, you typically have one recovering from the same, while another prepares to take its place).

It may also be time to consider raising auxiliary forces in Iraq to lessen the burden on our troops. (The Kurdish peshmerga are a ready-made one, though the use of an ethnic minority to maintain order in a conquered country carries its own risks).

Admittedly, the use of foreign auxiliaries trained and even officered by Americans would be a measure troublingly redolent of empire. And it's one that would make explicit all the issues about post-liberation Iraq that seem to have received bizarrely inadequate consideration from the Pentagon (even given

that the war ended several weeks earlier than plan-
ners expected).

An alternative would be to subsidize the tempo-
rary deployment of friendly forces to help police Iraq.
(Apparently, Washington has already approached
India on this). This, too, would entail political risk.

In the meantime, however, the Pentagon should
do right by the division that took Baghdad – and let
it come home to enjoy the appreciation of the
American people for a stunning victory.

Even though we as a family figured he wouldn't be home until the fall, seeing it in print was a reality check I could've lived without. I whole-heartedly agreed with Mr. Foreman and I sent him a letter stating so. It was published with many other letters on June 20th. I was impressed that my letter was mean-ingful enough to have a space in a newspaper with the reader-ship of the Post.

Many months later the article Mr. Foreman wrote would lend itself to a moment of six degrees of separation for another woman Jo Caldwell and myself. I sent Mr. Foreman an email telling him of our chance encounter. I hope he enjoyed the story as much as we did. (See appendix for email to Foreman). Jo and I met at Erik Kukkonen's homecoming months after Sean came home. Jo's son served with Erik in the 82nd Airborne. As it turns out we each wrote a letter to the editor regarding Foreman's article and they were printed on the same day, on the same page. It was one of those unusual encounters in life that unexpectedly bring two strangers together. (The New York Post denied my request to reprint the letters to the editor)

I enjoyed meeting another mother who could get as fired up as me and then respond with a letter. When I wrote the letter to Foreman I was angry that the Army was putting the troops and their families through this emotional roller coaster. If I, as a mother, was this angry I couldn't begin to imagine what it was doing to the wives and children of the soldiers.

The roller coaster effect was compounded with the thought that if Tom's disease progressed rapidly and Sean wasn't home for five or six more months how would I break the news to him. I couldn't help but wonder how Sean was going to handle the decline of his live action hero. At this point I was beginning to feel a crisis in the making. I've learned over the years it is far better to be proactive than to sit and wait for disaster to find me. I started investigating the steps I should be taking.

I needed to talk to someone from the base to help me figure out the process for getting a soldier home due to a family crisis. I wasn't even sure how the Army defined a family crisis. I phoned Ft. Stewart and spoke to a variety of people. Through them I found out that there is a Family Readiness Group (FRG) that has a leader for each platoon. Through the FRG leader the family can find out good information like where the platoon is, when they may be coming home and networking with other Army families. I wish I had known of them earlier.

I found out Tom's condition would not warrant Sean coming home any sooner. Family members have to be close to death before a soldier is granted permission to come home. Yet the advice I received from the non-commissioned officers I spoke with at Ft. Stewart was great. They felt I should let Sean's company commander know about Tom's health issue. If Tom had a significant deterioration and we decided to let Sean know, the American Red Cross would deliver the message. By informing the company commander ahead of time he would be prepared to assist Sean with concerns he may have and make sure he had access to the chaplain. There was a lot to consider. In the end I decided to hold back on doing anything until I felt more certain of Tom's condition. By this time Tom was scheduled for a September appointment at the center in Charlotte. If Sean was still not home and the diagnosis was ALS then I would re-visit my options. Fortunately, I never had to make that decision.

The more I thought about Tom's health the more it broke my heart. One night Kate came into my bedroom to say good-night and after she left I lay there thinking about both the kids and how they would handle this new situation. As I lay there thinking about all of the areas of our life that would be affected by a diagnosis of ALS I burst into tears. Would Tom be there for Kate when she got married and had children? How would Sean handle surviving a war only to find his best friend, the one who gave it to him straight 100% of the time, and, most importantly, his hero was dying? Then the most awful thought of all crossed my mind; how can I possibly take the loss of my soul mate? It was more than I could bear to think about and yet it was all I could think about. These thoughts became a loop tape in my mind and the more the tape played the more I wept. At midnight I crawled out of bed and went downstairs to sit with Tom. We talked on the back porch so Kate wouldn't hear us. It must have been difficult for him that night since I cried as I have never cried in my life. I told him I wasn't ready for this to happen. We had just entered a great time in our life together. With the kids moving on we were experiencing freedoms together we hadn't known for years. Even with all that we had been through the last 10 years this was the first time I'd felt that life wasn't fair and I expressed this to Tom. We had lost babies, his health and career were shot to hell, and our son was still in a dangerous situation, it just didn't seem right to have to face another life challenge that could be so devastating. We had always been able to put a positive spin on our problems, to make the most out of things, yet this seemed insurmountable. It was the first time that I hated what we were going through. I cried and I talked while Tom listened until four o'clock in the morning. To this day I don't know how Tom was able to comfort me when he was feeling so threatened himself. I don't know anyone who can put others before himself like Tom.

Since the earliest appointment I could get at the Carolinas ALS Center was September and my breakdown happened at the end of July we were going to have wait; I would allow myself this one time emotional indulgence and then put those emotions on a shelve. I was certain I could retrieve them if necessary.

Because we were tired of being by ourselves Tom, Kate and

I went to my mom and dad's in Florida for the 4th of July holiday. The three of us needed some tender loving care and my parent's were just the ones to give it to us. They are the best when it comes to taking care of their family. From the minute we arrived to the minute we were leaving they enveloped us in their love and care.

While we were there Sean called a few times and, once again, thanks to call forwarding we didn't miss any of his calls. He made those calls using a satellite phone and talked to us for a good half hour. He told us that it looked like the 3rd ID would be home by the end of July. Even though we reminded him that the dates were fluid (we also reminded him of our plan to count on him coming home in the fall), it didn't matter, he still was excited that this time it was for real and he felt sure he would be home in time for our family vacation. I hoped, for his sanity, that this time it was true.

His calls were coming with more frequency now that he had a satellite phone to use. Another wonderful advantage of this phone was that there wasn't the delay we had been experiencing with the pay phone.

The second week of July we received another letter.

> *06/17/03*
>
> *Well I haven't written in awhile, I'm not sure how to explain it. Its kinda hard sometimes to find the motivation to write home, its nothing personal, you just get sick of writing. Recently I had the opportunity to use the phone two times, and I couldn't get through, I must have dialed for forty five minutes straight, I was ready to flip out on someone, especially those POG's that wait in line behind you and give you attitude about being on the phone for too long. Me and Burress went this morning at 0330 to try to get through no such luck. At least you guys know we are trying to call you.*
>
> *Foolojah, or whatever, isn't all its cracked up to*

be. I'll start with where we are right now. CCO 3/15 1 and third platoons are located in a 1 mile square compound that used maintain BMP's in. there's a greater outer wall outside that, I'm not sure the dimensions, 800 meters maybe, and the entire compound used to be for the 14th Medina Division and is now home to us and a part of the Mujahadean training camp comprised of mainly women. Cool background if you ask me.

Weather, its about 117 degrees by 10:00 in the morning and a steady 120 degrees till about 8:00 at night. Our uniform was finally downgraded to boomy cap + t shirt and weapon, which is nice b/c that DCU top was becoming so tortuously hot I didn't even want to go take a leak b/c I would have to put it on. We are fortunate enough to have shelter from the blazing sun. Its like a prison compound you would see on a French Island out on the ocean somewhere, bars on windows, 1 story ranch style house w/high ceiling concrete porch surrounding whole buildings. there's separate buildings all connected by the raised concrete porch, three separate buildings to be exact. One building holds Red platoon (first) the next our tankers we are attached to, and finally Blue (third). there's nothing inside, concrete floor, no power, nothing. Just dirt on the outside and like 8 or 9 scattered trees. I like it. It reminds me of what the old west would look and feel like.

There are ice runs available daily so at least we have something cold to drink everyday. Its become a lot like Ft. Stewart, PT 0600 – 0700 Mon – Fri Sat Sun off, can wear PTs on Sun all day if you want and we do like a half hour training on perishable skills sometimes b/w 0800 and 1100.

The days are very slow and relaxed, missions are rare and there's lots of time to sleep and write, which I'm going to catch up on both.

I got the letter telling me about your Sig P220 (I think that's the right nomenclature), that's the last thing I got from you guys. Aunt Jess sent me a box that was a big hit with the guys and me – we ate all the brownies within minutes. The box Mom and Kate sent I horded for myself, and let me tell you, the milk was outstanding, especially iced down and the cookies hit the spot. Thank Nanna & Pop PoP for their box it had exactly the right things.

As far as action, well before I forget to tell you we had our own CIB ceremony over here, I got good pictures of everything so don't worry. I also heard the ceremony is going to be redone once we get to the states. You were right Dad, I was moved to tears streaming down my face as the national anthem played, or was sung. Its funny how you knew that would happen.

As far as action goes, not much, actually none. On our foot patrols through the city two packs of dogs followed us the whole time – just barking and howling the whole click. I wasn't sure what the ROE was on barking dogs, so I didn't slaughter them into oblivion like they deserve.

We traded members of our team w/red platoon. We got Dudley a 22 yr old Ranger stud who already got his CIB in Afghanistan w/the first Ranger Bat. We got rid of Mantle, he was dead wood. Now we have 2 two o three's and a SAW and a rifleman as our team, I'm convinced we have the most lethal team in the Company with the most true combat action between the four of us.

I don't know about awards I could find out what I'm getting, if anything at all, but I want to wait till the ceremony, which was supposed to be over here three days ago but it got delayed indefinitely.

Our former (former because we just got a new one two days ago) CO got awarded w/a silver star and a bronze star.

I'm still trying to go to sniper school when I get back, that's on the top of my list, and then probably Special Forces school. We'll see how things turn out. I also heard that the Army is looking for guys to go to Korea when we get back, I'm gonna volunteer if the opportunity should arise. Its only one year deployment, and I would like to go overseas again and see the East. You get a lot of time to think ahead so all you do is plan ahead, you know?

An explosion just went off that rivals anything any civilian would have felt, Dad would know, like air strikes you used to call in. EOD blows stuff (mines) everyday, twice a day one right after another. The explosions cause a shockwave that kicks up strong winds across the desert and causes small tornadoes to occur as a result, I really should get a photo of one one time. I need a photo of the ORO blowing up also.

Well I guess I'll go now. Its about 1330 and I need a drink, plus radio watch is coming up soon, so when I think of something good to write about, I will. Keep in touch, no I didn't forget bout you guys. I'm gonna work on Kates letter next.

Love, Sean
"A ROCKHARD SOLDIER"
- CHARLIE ROCK -

By the time we received both this letter and the next one we had spoken to Sean a few times. We were caught up on where he was and how he was doing simply because he was calling us. Yet, we never tired of reading every word he wrote. We hadn't spoken to him much in June so the letters helped to fill in details about some of his experiences that there wasn't enough

Sean smoking a cigar and cleaning his weapon in Falluja.

Sean and Burress (the one Sean refers to in his last few letters home) right after the CIB ceremony.

This is the CIB ceremony for 3rd platoon Charlie Company. Sean is getting his CIB pinned on him in this photograph.

time for over the phone.

This is the last letter he wrote from Iraq:

06/21

We got a satellite phone today, that means at anytime of the day, any day of the week, I can call you guys. A few of us chipped in b/c one phone costs 650 dollars. A phone card, 80 minutes worth costs 82 dollars. Sounds expensive, but worth it. Soon enough, like tomorrow I'll be able to call you guys. I figure I'll pick one day of the week b/w two times to call all the time, probably Sunday. We totally have off on Sundays. I'll have to see how it goes.

Got your letter today Dad, sounds like you like your SIG. Send some photos I can't picture what it looks like right now. Hey Dad, send a shotgun news if you can as well, I need some eye candy.

I don't hold the squad leader position anymore, that was temporary, our new SL is SSG Albright. He's much better than SGT Hernandez. I don't know about awards, I don't wanna ask. I'd just rather find out what I'm getting at the awards ceremony. I think from what I hear that's going to be stateside.

I'm already getting back in shape, so that's good. I figure if I'm not where I want to be by the time I get back I won't have very far to go at least. Right now, however, I'm battling a raging stomach virus – the works. I'm not sure how I got it, but probably had to do w/the fact that Munoz unknowingly filled a water bottle up w/non-potable water, and I drank some. I suspect it will be gone in a few days from now.

I'm going to be honest, there is no point in keeping as many troops here as they did. I could see one brigade, but not two. There isn't even anyone here to fight under conventional warfare. Well, I know that a brigade Commander is coming out here to assess our situation to see if our brigade needs to stay here or if he can send us home. I don't have much confidence in the higher ups to send us home. I'm not expecting to go home any sooner than September No matter what, I don't need my hopes shattered again, you know?

That's it, I'm gonna go now. Keep sending cigars, there nice when you have some time to daydream – any kind, the same kind – different kinds, humor me. I read in the paper Jen is home – or the band is home, so I would naturally assume that Jen is included. I gave her your # so maybe she'll call – I would doubt it but you never know. I wish I had her cell # still I'd call it and see whats up. Ok, take care chill out.

Sean
A Rock Hard Soldier
Charlie Rock

In this letter Sean mentions SSGT Albright. Interestingly when we received this letter I had just made contact with Albright's wife, Shanna. It turned out that she was our FRG leader. She was absolutely wonderful in every way. Shanna assured me that if we needed to get a message to Sean or his CO that she would be able to help me each step of the way. She also assured me that she would let us know when they were coming home as soon as she knew. Additionally, we received group emails from her each time she received new information.

By mid-July we knew Sean wouldn't be home in time for the family vacation. For a day or two the news we received indicated he might come home while we were on vacation. This set us off trying to figure out whether or not we should cancel the trip. We were confused about what we should do. The complication for us was the vacation location. At home in Durham we could

This is the photograph Sean sent home right after MOUT exercises in Kuwait. It is of the 3rd platoon, Charlie Company.

This is what Sean's sees when he looks down the barrel of his machine gun. At the edge of the tree line is an Iraqi bunker.

This was taken by Sean shortly after the firefight he writes about in his last few letters. The guard rail is the one that was hit by the Iraqi sniper.

get to Ft. Stewart in five hours. Once the 3rd ID left Kuwait Shanna would call us and that would give us a twelve-hour window to get ourselves to the base. So what to do? It would easily take us fifteen hours to get from Lake George to the base. Before I made any rash decisions to cancel our trip I waited the Army out.

The third Saturday in July Sean called about 10 a.m. eastern daylight time. He talked for an hour about the food, living conditions and missing life in the United States. But the main reason for his call was because he said a general told them that they would be coming home within two weeks. He believed the general as did we. Tom and I talked about it that evening and decided that on Sunday we would cancel our vacation reservations.

At 6:30 the next morning Sean called again. This time he called to tell me that they had been told that they not only would not be home anytime soon but that it would be the end of September or even October before they received redeployment orders. He was angry and although I felt badly for him I was glad I hadn't had a chance to cancel our reservations. It would have added insult to injury. He asked that I send him a CD player, CD's and his Playstation. The call lasted only a few minutes. Of course we put everything together for him within a few days. Just before we mailed the package we received a call from Shanna telling us that they would home by early August. This time it was for sure. As difficult as it was to believe, she convinced us it was definite. We held off mailing the items Sean requested since we didn't want them to get lost in transition. We began to put our energy into preparing for his much-anticipated homecoming.

V.

COMING HOME

THE LAST WEEK OF JULY, TOM, KATE AND I MET MY FAMILY at The Sagamore resort in Lake George, NY. Every few years my parents, my two brothers and my sister along with their families get together for a family reunion. Since some of us live in different states it's a great way to stay connected.

I brought my laptop computer to maintain my access to the Internet and read my email while I was on vacation. I didn't want to miss any messages from Shanna. By this time we were as close to certain as we could be that the 3rd ID was coming home in early August.

On Wednesday, July 31 I received an email from Shanna confirming that 3-15 Charlie Company was in Kuwait. I was elated! As much as I wanted to see Sean, that desire paled compared to knowing that he was finally physically safe; I was in such high spirits that I could barely contain myself.

After reading Shanna's email I sat down and composed a statement to read to my family that evening in the dining hall. I thanked them for their support and encouragement to Sean, Tom, Kate and I during this stressful period in our lives. Then I read a portion of an article Shanna had forwarded to the families written by Col. Joseph P. DiSalvo, 2nd BCT commander on July 28, 2003 telling the families their soldiers were on the way home and they would be in Kuwait within days. Even though the expectation was that the entire brigade would be in Kuwait by August 2, the information she received was that our unit was already there.

As I finished up my talk I ended with the phrase that "Sean was now in the safest place he had been in since March 19th."

By the time I finished reading there wasn't a dry eye in the room. I surprised them with the good news. I went on to tell them that we had confirmation that Sean was in Kuwait. At this point I heard my sister, Jess, and Kate begin to sob. As I looked around at the kids, Sean's cousins, they were grinning from ear to ear with tears in their eyes. It was a wonderful moment for all of us!

Many members of my family had stepped up to provide support to Sean and to us. Some of his cousins wrote him letters and sent him packages. His cousin closest in age, Matthew, wrote him a few times and sent him his prom picture. Sean held onto the photograph and kept it with his personal belongings. Sean's cousins in California sent him packages and letters on a regular basis.

My sister's daughters received postcards from Sean. The youngest, Kelly, brought one to school for show and tell. She also took to reading it out loud at the dinner table each night for weeks. The girls took the photograph of Sean that was on the Internet with them to school in their backpacks every day.

My brother, Kevin, and I spoke on the phone a number of times. Once in a while he called me in the morning at work to check in on me. His entire church prayed for Sean on a weekly basis. One of his nieces from his wife's family dedicated her 16th birthday to Sean. Kevin was terrific at spreading the word and encouraging those around him to remember Sean in their daily prayers.

My sister-in-law Kathy and nephew Jonathon sent packages and magazines. Sean always appreciated the magazines and anything that would help to curb the boredom. When Jonathon had his class photograph taken they all signed it and sent Sean a copy.

One of the more poignant letters of support that Sean received was from his grandpa, my dad. In all of the years I have known my dad he has not been much of a letter writer.

My dad was torn up over his grandson being in a war zone. He knew that Sean needed to hear from all of us and he realized how important it was for Sean to receive letters from home. In many ways letters to a loved one in war are a way of sharing hugs long distance; they serve to tell the person we are writing to they are worth the time and effort it takes to compose a letter. Phone calls are easy but letters require thought and energy. Dad wrote a newsletter (See appendix) about our extended family's activities and a cover letter. As far as I am concerned, this letter my dad wrote to Sean was one of his finest moments:

> *3/27/03*
> *Sean*
>   *Attached is my first attempt in writing a newsletter – I was inspired by you & only you – Keep in mind I'm a poor speller & certainly not a great letter writer – However I thought I'd give it a try – writing letters & long notes is like going to the dentist – but I struggled through it & I hope you get the idea how we feel about you and to give you a little information about the family. If I forget anyone I'll be better the next time – maybe the war will be over and I won't have to do it –*
>   *Lots of love –*
>   *Grandpa & the rest of the family*

I include the letter from my father as an illustration of how deeply people are affected by the involvement of their loved ones in a war. It wasn't just Tom, Kate and I who were both proud of our infantryman and worried constantly about his safety. It was all the people we were connected to. Our families took time out of their busy lives and made it a priority to find time for Sean. Sean is aware of each and every one of the people in his life that remembered him by sending him letters and packages; each one eased his days. Their actions helped to relieve some of the burden from us financially and emotionally. Tom's parents and his sister, Kathleen, sent him cards and supplies. His sister's church remembered him at mass every Sunday. My sister Jess regularly sent him packages of home baked goods, as did many people in her office. Sean was and is eternally grateful for their support.

It was with this commitment and support from my family that I shared our welcome news that he would be home sooner rather than later. It was special that we were all together for this piece of very good news.

We left The Sagamore on August 3rd. As we were packing up to go Kate's eyes filled with tears. I thought that she was sad we were leaving the family and didn't want to say goodbye. I asked her what was wrong and as we started to talk she told me saying goodbye was not an issue, she was upset because Tom's declining strength was apparent to her on this trip. She had to help him open the sliding glass doors to the porch or carry heavy packages the whole week. She could also see the constant twitching of the muscles in his arms. A few weeks earlier I told her what I knew about Tom' condition but it didn't seem to sink in right away. It was a difficult day for her.

I knew what she was going through because of my previous breakdown. I realized then that we were beginning to grieve. There isn't much you can say or do for someone who is feeling this way except be there for them. Of course on the way home from the airport every song on the radio was one of those sappy sad songs that just prompted her to cry more.

The good thing about a breakdown is that once you let it happen it doesn't come back with quite the same vengeance. It's not as if you don't feel the continued loss but the intensity isn't quite as strong. It was better that it happened when I was there for her instead of when she was back at school. By the next day Kate began to focus on the positive and got busy making big welcome home signs for Sean. It was time to re-focus our energies.

I hadn't realized the effect that our family's saga had on others until the week before Sean came home. The week was full of ups and downs and was difficult on everyone. We weren't sure from hour to hour the day Sean's unit was expected. My parents had to rearrange their travel plans if they were going to be there with us at Ft. Stewart. I had to arrange for time off from work. Even the family Kate was babysitting for chipped in and worked with her regarding her availability. It couldn't have been easy for them as both of the parents were working and one of them had to keep changing their schedule until we were certain of the day we had to leave. Yet, not once did they make Kate uncomfortable, in fact, quite the opposite, they were thrilled to know he was coming home.

At 5 p.m. August 5th Shanna Albright called to tell me that being in Savannah on the 6th would be a really good idea. She did not have any news that she could officially share but she assured us that if we were there by the 6th we would not miss anything. That was all I needed to rejoice. We couldn't contain ourselves; we blasted the music, we danced in the kitchen and smiled until our faces hurt.

Within an hour of the call from Shanna Sean called too. He wasn't sure what day he would fly out on but felt sure it was soon. He was bubbling over with excitement. He told us he had driven one of the 5-ton trucks down Highway One from Falluja to Kuwait. He was thrilled to be eating good food like a sandwich from the Subway shop in Camp New York.

We quickly got ourselves together and drove down to Savannah on August 6th. At the same time my mom and dad left their home in Florida to meet us there. Since Jerry and Vicki Kiernan's son was due to come home that week they met us there too. That week our cell phone bills were out of control. We were in constant touch with every one we knew.

Once I got off the highway I got lost looking for the hotel in Savannah and called Shanna for directions. We were going to have dinner with her so she was waiting for us in the hotel parking lot. I had also called Jerry to tell him that we made a wrong turn and were going to be a few minutes late. It was then that I realized that I never told him that both Shanna and my parents were waiting at the same hotel. Jerry could have organized it so all of them could hang out in the hotel lobby and wait together.

When we pulled up to the hotel we finally met Shanna face to face. Even though we had never met it was like seeing an old friend. When we entered the lobby we found Jerry and Vicki sitting right next to my dad. But of course they didn't talk to each other because they had never met before. All of them were waiting on us only they didn't know it. Apparently they had all been there for an hour or more. We all had a good laugh over it.

Dinner was fantastic. We talked non-stop. The excitement of seeing our loved ones soon was palpable. The hotels were filled to the brim with families waiting for their soldiers and the sense of anticipation was highly emotional. It felt like all the best Christmas mornings of your life packed into one.

We spent Thursday, August 7th in downtown Savannah. It was a good opportunity to just take a deep breath and relax for a bit. By then we were feeling good that Sean was arriving sometime on the 8th yet we wouldn't truly believe it until we had final confirmation of their departure.

Shanna called at 11:55 p.m. on the 7th to tell us that Sean was in Germany. He would definitely be home on the 8th. Without a doubt, no delays, no monkey business, for sure he would be home on Friday.

ON AUGUST 8, 2003 we woke up with a great sense of excitement. We called Jerry and Vicki to let them know that Sean was on his way and invited them to join us at Ft. Stewart. My parents, Tom, Kate and I headed over to Hinesville, the town right outside the base, for breakfast with some of the other 3rd ID families. Shanna had arranged a final time for us to meet and chat before our soldiers came home. Some of the families had been there for days and they came from as far away as Arizona and Texas. They had come early because they were determined to be there for their soldier's homecoming.

Later on I thought about the expenses involved in a homecoming like this. There must have been many families that couldn't afford the associated costs of a trip of this magnitude, i.e., airfare, hotel costs, eating out, etc. It must have been difficult for many of the families to miss this event and equally so for the soldiers who didn't have anyone to greet them. If you are one of those family members be assured many people that day greeted your soldier and thanked them for their service. I know Vicki and Jerry reached out to as many as they could even as they yearned for their own son's return.

We arrived at the field by 9:30 a.m. My dad, Tom and Kate were in charge of getting ice, soda, water and sandwiches. My dad made sure we were set for the day. We set ourselves up alongside the bleachers as close to the field as we could get.

By 10 a.m. the sun was shining, the temperature was rising and the humidity was coming on with a vengeance. I worried about my parents being able to take a day of this kind of weather without any shelter. We had an umbrella and chairs but that didn't come close to the cool air-conditioned house they were use to. Initially we were told Sean would be on one of the first flights in, however, it turns out he was one of the last. If we had known that in advance we wouldn't have changed a thing. We would have all stayed just to watch the other troops arrive!

The troops flew in to Hunter Army Airbase where they turned in their weapons and boarded a bus for the 40-minute drive to Ft. Stewart. We were able to follow their movements via public announcements to the families waiting at Ft. Stewart. It was a fantastic way to get us charged up. The announcer would name the unit that had landed and then say "company xxx is now at Hunter", a few minutes later he would inform us "they have boarded the bus". The families would cheer with each piece of information. We were told when the unit had entered the gates of Ft. Stewart, when they were a mile away, and then 2 blocks away. Before you knew it there was the bus. Even if your soldier wasn't on that bus you hugged those around you whether you knew them or not.

The bus parked on the opposite side of the field, the men unloaded and then marched on to the field. An Army officer spoke a few words; the Army band played two short songs and the men were officially dismissed. The crowd surged onto the field searching for their loved ones. It was a sea of hugs, kisses, couples clinging to each other, kids hanging on to dads, mom's and dad's delighted over the save return of their sons. It was a moment no one will surely forget.

We watched this scene repeated all day. I don't remember how many units came in before Sean's but each welcome was as powerful as the last.

While we waited we introduced ourselves to the news crew covering the homecoming. MSNBC and CNN were two of the stations present at the event. As luck would have it, these stations had set themselves up near where we were camping out.

Tom noticed the MSNBC trailer and wondered who was covering the event. He thought maybe Brian Williams would be since the 3rd Infantry came to his rescue the previous March. He encouraged me to go find out, and so I did. I knocked on the trailer door. The man (I never did get his name) who answered was enthusiastic when I told him that Sean was in the area the day the helicopter went down. He told me that Justin Balding, a producer for a number of programs for NBC, who was also on the helicopter with Williams, was at the homecoming. He asked me not to go anywhere and told me that he wanted to connect me with Mr. Balding. He then changed his mind and asked me to go with him as he looked for Justin. I think he feared that if I left he wouldn't find me again. Off I went with him. By now it was about 11:00 in the morning and getting to the hottest part of the day and here we are jogging looking for Justin Balding. I had no idea where we were going all I knew was that the both of us started sweating like crazy. We were drenched by the time we finally caught up with Balding.

Mr. Balding was more than happy to talk to me. I introduced him to my family and to the Kiernan's. Shortly after the introductions Craig White, David Bloom's cameraman, came over. We were all surprised that these men were taking the time to speak to us. Craig and Justin were kind and thoughtful in what they shared with us.

Justin spoke highly of the 3rd Infantry. He was impressed with the troops and their ability to stay focused. We didn't know much about the helicopter incident except what Brian William's had reported on the NBC Nightly News, and the scant details Sean wrote home about. Justin told us the helicopter that he was in with anchorman Brian Williams and General Wayne Downing (retired) was shot at by Iraqi's; it was an unforeseen and frightening event. The Chinook they were flying in took a rocket propelled grenade (RPG) and an AK-47 in the cockpit requiring them to land unexpectedly. Much to their relief the 3d Platoon, C Company, 3rd Battalion, 15th Infantry was there to surround the downed helicopters. Due to one of the sand storms we heard so much about they were stuck there for a couple of days. During this time Mr. William's suggested that the soldiers write letters home and told them that he would be sure their families received them quickly.

Jerry, Vicki, Tom and I spent hours talking with Justin and Craig in the hot sun. I briefly remember thinking that as hot as it was and as sweaty as we were it didn't dampen the enthusiasm of any of us.

What we received from talking to these two men was the sense of what our sons had been through. In a way they prepared us for what to expect from our sons. We listened to their experiences and perceptions of the war and took it to heart. They told us it took time for them to process what they had been through and that our kids had been through even more. It was reassuring to have someone give us some idea of what to expect. Yet as much as they told us it wasn't enough to prepare us for the difficulties of coming home from war.

As we spoke with Justin and Craig, Donna Gregory, the newswoman for MSNBC came over to introduce herself to us. Donna and I discovered that she lived just south of us in the Raleigh area and that we both knew Tracey Koepke, senior medical writer, for Duke University Medical Center. That was a fun coincidence to discover.

Me holding one of the signs Kate made.

Dad, Portia and Tom finding some shade to keep cool while the waiting continued.

Donna asked me to tell her about Sean and what the link was with Justin Balding and Brian Williams. I was happy to. Now that it was over and he was on his way home I felt it was good to share his story. When I finished she asked me if she could interview me as part of the homecoming coverage. Even though I was feeling a bit ragged looking I agreed. It was a wonderful event to share on TV. Donna had first decided to tape our interview and then for reasons I am unsure of she decided to do it live. I was surprised by her request and then a little intimidated by it but I agreed and felt good when it turned out to be an enjoyable experience.

In the meantime Tom's mom and dad were home in Niantic, Connecticut watching MSNBC hoping to get a glimpse of us or, even better yet, Sean. As they finished discussing the chance of that happening, there I was on their TV screen. For Tom's parents who were not in any condition to travel seeing that interview made their day. As it turns out some of our friends in New York saw the broadcast too.

It was a day to remember for many reasons. We met good and kind people that day. From TV broadcasters to citizens without arriving soldiers, people came from all over to welcome home the troops. We watched as people reunited throughout the day and cried with all of them. I marveled at my mother and father's strength to stay the course and not complain even once about the heat, humidity and over all lack of comfort. They wouldn't have missed this day for the world and to ease my mind they told me that repeatedly. It meant a lot to me to share the day with them.

Around 3:45 it was announced the plane carrying Task Force (T/F) 1-64 had landed at Hunter. Sean's unit was attached to the T/F 1-64. He was on the ground; he was finally in the United States of America. We were overwhelmed with excitement. There were hundreds of people there on the field chanting "USA, USA, USA" when they heard the announcement. No other welcome that day had the level of intensity of this one. Maybe it was because we had expected them earlier in the day or maybe it was because we all knew about the arduous battle T/F 1-64 endured taking Baghdad. To this day, I haven't figured out the reason for the difference but I can say this crowd was unsurpassed in its passion to welcome home the troops.

The crowd went crazy again when the announcement came that they were on the bus and heading to Ft. Stewart. I called my sister and the both of us cried. She could barely hear me with all the noise in the background.

Approximately 40 minutes later it was announced that T/F 1-64 had entered the gates of Ft. Stewart. Again the crowd erupted with "USA" chants. The announcer began to tell us how close they were by naming the streets that the bus passed. As it came into sight men and children ran alongside it. Tom was one of those men running alongside the bus. I have rarely seen him display this much enthusiasm. The crowd pushed beyond the roped off area cheering and chanting for their men.

The soldiers marched on to the field and were officially welcomed home. The band played a song or two and then the men were released to their families. We found Sean within minutes. Tom, Kate and I ran to him and hugged him fiercely. But perhaps the most touching moment for me was when my dad hugged Sean. He wept like a baby. The only times in my life that I witnessed tears in my dad eyes was when my mom had a car accident with Jessica and I in the car when we were kids and the day I married Tom. This day, the day his grandson came home from war overwhelmed him. My dad has said over and over that this was the best day of his life.

As we walked off the field we passed by the MSNBC tent. Donna Gregory was sitting on a box weeping just like the rest of us. I introduced her to Sean. I felt that I wanted her to meet this great young man I call my son. Before I knew it they had the lights and camera on and she was interviewing him! I stood next to him holding onto his arm the entire time.

All I could think was that he hadn't had a chance to catch his breath and he must think I'd totally lost my mind. As he spoke I didn't let go of him. For some reason, I felt like I was sending

Top to bottom: *Shanna Albright, Kate, Tom, Mary (me), my mom Carol and my dad John shielding ourselves from the sun while we waited for the troops to come home.*

Sean minutes after we welcomed him home.

Donna Gregory of MSNBC interviewing Sean.

him a message of calmness through my touch. After the interview, the anchorman remarked on air that it was sweet that I
didn't want to let go of him when in reality I was really thinking "Oh my God I can't believe he is being interviewed minutes
after he arrived!"

Donna asked him all the same questions she had asked me.
At the time, I was wondering if we would have the same
answers. For a minute there I felt as though I was on one of
those reality shows where they ask a family member how the
other family member responded to a question when they
weren't there. If they get the right answer they win something.
Only this was different, this was a live interview; I didn't want
us to sound ridiculous. She asked him "Why did you join the
Army?" and the whole time I'm thinking, it was because of 9/11,
right? I mean that is what he did, right? I sure hope so since that
is what I said in my interview. I questioned whether or not I
really knew the reason he joined the Army. This all went
through my mind in seconds. But Sean answered almost exactly as I had right down to the answer to "How have you changed
as a result of your experience?" We both said "more mature". I
was relieved when it was over and we could get back to the business of reuniting with Sean.

Sean's interview aired about 5:00 p.m. and again Tom's parents were watching MSNBC at just the right time. It was wonderful that they were able to see their grandson come home
even though they couldn't be there. Back in Cornwall a friend
of Sean's mother taped his interview. The kids up there got a
kick out of watching the tape. Seeing him interviewed was good
for them.

The first day and a half he was home, Sean was edgy but talk-
ative. He responded best to questions from my mom and dad.
Tom and I didn't ask him too much; somehow it didn't seem right
yet. His demeanor was good but not the Sean we knew. When he
sat down his legs were in a constant state of motion and he kept
his eye on the door most of the time. I suspected he needed some
time alone and that too much time with us would overwhelm

him. We, of course, wanted to be with him all day and all night. Fortunately for Sean's state of mind that was impossible since we were in a hotel and he was in his barracks. I really wanted to mother him, take him home and cook him meals.

By Sunday I was emotionally spent and so was he. My parents' left in the morning and it was time for us to figure out how to do this without them. About an hour after my parents had gone Sean got up, said goodbye and left without any further discussion as to when we would see him again. Since I had to leave the next morning to get back to work I figured that I wouldn't see him again until he came home on leave. I was devastated, so was Tom. We sat outside in the parking lot under a tree and had an emotional discussion on what to do next. Our hearts were broken, we didn't know what to do or say to our son. We felt helpless. We wanted him to have the space he needed yet we had the additional pressure of knowing that I had to leave the next day. We knew Sean was not thinking that far out.

To minimize the emotional damage I called Sean and arranged for us to meet him at the base later on that day. The telephone as a communication tool has always worked well for Sean and I. I shared my concerns and he shared his. He explained that he was on stimulation overload and more importantly that he needed time to adjust to living in a civilized world again rather than the world of the infantry all day, every day.

We would have benefited from having an authority share with us that the difficulties we were encountering were normal. We were taking his reactions personally and shouldn't have. Had I known then what I know now I would have been much more understanding. In fact, it is likely I would have encouraged him to have more time to himself.

I had a vision that it would all be okay right away that life would continue as we knew it before the war. Maybe he did too. We didn't realize the many barriers we would encounter. But we worked together; all four of us, to figure it out and come together as a family again.

We met Sean for breakfast before we left Georgia. Outside

the restaurant we ran into Justin Balding. He joined us and whether he knew it or not helped to ease the way for us all just a little bit. It seemed that the psychology of a successful homecoming for Sean would require the presence of other people when he was with us, at least for a little while. After breakfast we said goodbye knowing we would see Sean again in a week or so. In the end our struggles were worth it, Sean was home safely and that was all that mattered.

Sean had nearly three weeks of leave. That was a lot of time for him to fill with us. He was use to hanging around with his buddies and working long hours. After a week or so with us he went to visit his friends in Cornwall. While he was there the fire department gave a dinner in his and Sean Kiernan's honor. They surprised him with the party and a plaque thanking him for his service to the country.

When Sean came back from Cornwall he was invited to speak at a luncheon at the Duke Eye Center. One of the administrators, Brett Moran, had extended the invitation. Brett had often asked me about Sean and was a big supporter of the troops. He thought the staff would find it interesting to hear of Sean's experiences. Sean brought with him the artifacts and map he had from Iraq. He used the map to guide him in his description of the artifacts and his time in Iraq. He spoke uninterrupted for nearly 30 minutes then answered questions with as much honesty and integrity as the situation would allow for. It was a good cleansing experience for Sean to talk openly about the war and begin to process what he had been through.

A few days after Sean came home on leave we received a final letter although it wasn't from him. This letter was from his platoon leader, SFC Timothy Terpak.

Last letter home:
Although this letter is addressed to us, every soldier's family in SFC Terpak's platoon received the same letter personally addressed to them.

14 August 2003

This letter was originally written at the Al Rasheed Hotel in Baghdad on 27 April 2003. I intended to send this letter to inform you of your son's actions. However, after talking to my squad leaders and company commander, I was advised not to send the letter until we were safely in the United States. The reasoning was that the letter may have inadvertently caused you to think something had happened to your son.

As I sit here and review the letter, I am still a very humbled man. Your son's actions and bravery were very instrumental in the overall success of the unit.

I hope you are as proud as I am of your son.
Sincerely,
Timothy Terpak
SFC, USA
Platoon Leader

SFC Timothy Terpak
1000 Sweetbriar Court
Hinesville, GA 31313

• • •

27 April 2003
Dear Mr. and Mrs. Ward,

I am writing this letter from Baghdad, Iraq, where my platoon is currently stabilizing a now liberated Iraqi people. The intent of this letter, is to tell of your son's bravery and courage under fire. It is my hope to accurately portray the actions of your son, displayed on the battlefield in the face of an armed enemy.

On 21 March 2003, the United States Army

conducted the longest, fastest and largest desert assault in history. Through technological advances in equipment, we were able to move rapidly through the open desert and into the urban terrain of An Najaf, Karbala and Baghdad. We were decisively and overwhelmingly successful. What we accomplished will be studied by military analysts and historians for generations. History was being made starting on this morning. This accomplishment was in no small part due to the efforts of your son.

On the morning of 21 March 2003, your son crossed the international border complex between Kuwait and Iraq, with the mission of freeing an oppressed people from a dictator who shows no compassion for his citizens. As we moved north, we encountered an armed force defending a critical objective. Without hesitation, your son performed his duties flawlessly. His actions enabled the platoon to complete its mission and do so without casualty. This feat is a direct result of the actions of your son. For in the Infantry, no single person is responsible for the overall success, it is the team, all 163 soldiers who complete the mission.

As we continued our push toward Baghdad, we continuously encountered armed resistance. Your son never wavered in the face of the enemy and his actions are in keeping with the finest traditions of the military service, and the Infantry, in particular. The Infantryman is a different breed of soldier. He trains all his career, to close with and destroy enemy forces with overwhelming firepower and superior equipment, readily willing to give his life, if necessary. At the same time, he prays he may never have to use his skills. Your son rose up to the challenge and came out victorious; a man of pride and honor; having accomplished something others will only read about in history books. You should share my pride in your son's accomplishments. As his platoon leader, it is my job to lead him into harm's way. To me, this is the most difficult aspect of being a leader of combat soldiers. However, your son, and his comrades, fought together and covered each other's back, ensuring mission accomplishment and the safety of every soldier.

I write this letter a very humbled man. Never did I think that we would be sitting here in Baghdad with every single soldier, all ten fingers and ten toes. Surely I thought someone would be injured, as it is the nature of ground combat. I stood in awe and watched your son and his very young platoon mates act without thinking, performing the tasks we trained so hard on for the previous six months and succeed far above even my expectations. Your son stands here proud and serves as a testament to the nations' will and the might of our brave servicemen and women. Your son volunteered to serve his country in a very difficult time, knowing very well he may be called into combat. Still he chose Infantry. This speaks volumes about the character of your son.

I cannot put to paper the emotions and fear shared with your son during this time. I also cannot accurately reflect the pride I have for your son. I hope this letter in some way does justice for the feeling I have for your son. He is truly an American Hero and you should be a very proud parent.

I hope to be able to return your son to you soon. We are currently expected to return to the United States somewhere near the end of May. With some maintenance on equipment, and other routine re-deployment tasks, your son should be on leave by the beginning of July. I can not guarantee this, but this is the truth as of today.

I will close now, again telling you how proud I am of your soldier and how privileged and honored I feel for having had the opportunity to serve with him on the field of battle.

Respectfully yours,

TIMOTHY TERPAK
SFC, USA
Platoon Leader

AFTERWARD

IT IS NEARLY A YEAR SINCE SEAN CAME HOME AND IT HAS BEEN GOOD. It has been good because we were one of the fortunate families to have their soldier return home. Tom, Sean, Kate and I are acutely aware that this story could have had a very different ending.

Kate is doing well. Her transfer went smoothly and she is entering her junior year. This summer she is busy working and socializing with new friends.

Tom's health condition has consumed much of our time this year. He continues to struggle with the deterioration of the strength in his arms. He has received a tenuous diagnosis of chronic demyelinating polyneuropathy disease (CIDP). CIDP is a non-acute form of Gullian Barre. His long-term prognosis remains unclear. Yet we know he doesn't have ALS and for that we are grateful.

Sean is still in the infantry and has recently been promoted to an E4. He is now Specialist Sean T. Ward. Since his return to Ft. Stewart he has learned how to drive the Bradley and that, for the moment, has become his new job. He still hopes to go to sniper school.

As it stands right now the 3rd ID has received orders to return to deploy to Iraq between November 2004 and February 2005 for an undetermined timeframe.

The past year has been a blessedly peaceful one for our family. Concerns I may have had prior to the war often seem insignificant to me now. Tom and I discovered we had to learn to love Sean unconditionally this year. Sean enjoyed it when we visited him at the base and yet he often went hours without speaking to us when we were with him. It wasn't that he wasn't talking to us; it was a quietness that came over him. We knew from the homecoming not to take it personally but rather to be supportive. He struggled with understanding his finances and other issues that come up now and then. He didn't hesitate to seek our help. We didn't judge or overreact; therefore, I think that helped him reach out whenever necessary. Adjusting to life in garrison after what he had been through took time, patience and love from each of us.

Sean was recently home on leave. He was with us for two weeks. Sean is finally at ease with us all of the time now. He is comfortable with who he is, where he's been in life and the mission that awaits him in the next year.

Appendix

The following are additional letters and writings from friends and family:

Were you ever young?
sometime before the weight of now?
When you knew for sure
the things you knew
and didn't know
what you couldn't do.
When you were young
Did you ever know?

By Tom Ward (Sean's Dad)
3/20/03

A letter we received from Erik Kukkonen:

June 7
Dear Mr. and Mrs. Ward
  Hey what's going on? I got your letter today from May 7. Its great to hear from you. And thanks for the advice. I was glad to call home and talk to my parents and hear that Sean was ok! I was so worried about him. Its kind of weird to think back to when me and Sean were younger and we use

to dream about going in the military and going to "war". And look now it really happened. Knowing what I know now I don't think I will ever wish to go to war again, it's not as fun as I imagined. So I heard Sean got a bronze star tell him I said congratulations. My unit also received CIB's and we got put in for Bronze Stars also, but don't know if we will get them. I have yet to run into Sean yet though. I am staying by BIA "Baghdad International Airport" in the city. We share the same sector. We also have done some raids with the 3rd ID. Way back in March my battalion got attached to the 75th ranger regiment and we went to Ar Ar Saudi Arabia to the Socom airbase. We were suppose to jump into BIA the night after the air war started but the "3rd ID" jumped the gun and went across the border without being told. So we didn't jump instead we went through and cleared the city they bypassed so the supply line would reach them, our biggest fights were in As Samawah, Diwania, and Falluja. Nobody heard to much about us because we didn't have reporters with us. We work with a lot of CAG guys "Delta and ODA teams" and they prohibited the camera guys. Well anyway tell Sean I said hi and I can't wait to see him. I have no clue when I will get home, but I will call him up as soon as I get back. Well thanks for the letter, hope all is going well for you and hopefully I will see you soon!
  Erik

Erik came home February 2004. Within a day of his arrival Sean was there to be with him. Sean and Erik did not receive the coveted bronze star. Sean received an Army Commendation Medal (ARCOM) and Erik received an ARCOM with a V (valor) device. Erik has re-enlisted for another four years and will serve with the 10th Mountain Division out of Ft. Drum, NY.

The email I sent to the New York Post after meeting Jo Caldwell:

> *The 3rd Infantry Division, the 82nd Airborne and*
> *Six degrees of Separation – February 1, 2004*
> *Dear Mr. Foreman,*
>
> *Back on June 16, 2003 you wrote a passionate article concerning the 3rd Infantry and their extended deployment in Iraq. As the mother of a 3rd Infantry soldier I wholeheartedly agreed with you and in fact sent a letter to the Post stating my position and concern. On June 20th the Post printed my letter and many other letters from concerned family members of our troops.*
>
> *It was thrilling to know that my words and thoughts found a voice through the Post. I've kept the article and the corresponding letters to the editor for our family for historical purposes. Yesterday my son's friend from high school came home from Iraq. Erik serves with the 82nd Airborne and has been there since the beginning of the war. My son Sean, traveled from Ft. Stewart to Ft. Bragg (about a 5 hour drive) on Friday to spend time with him. It was a fantastic moment for both of them, they worried about each other for the better part of a year.*
>
> *Of course Erik's family was there as well. They traveled from New York a week ago so they wouldn't miss the homecoming. We live in Durham, NC, having moved here a little over a year ago from NY so it was without question that we would go to Bragg to welcome Erik home. It was one of our greatest moments in life, second only to our son's return on August 8th, to have had the opportunity*

to be part of Erik's safe return to the United States.

One of Erik's very close friends in the 82nd came home with him. His name is Sean Caldwell. Sean's family was there as well. We were fortunate to meet their family. The three mom's – me, Erik's mom Debbie and Sean's mom, Jo, had a rather impromptu support group – "Mom's recovering from their son's return from war". Toward the end of our visit with the families yesterday Jo and I were discussing the ups and downs of the much-anticipated homecoming, you know, like the article you wrote are they? yes, this is the date, then no, this is the date and so on for months. For some reason I remembered the Post *article and started talking about it with Jo and when she said her letter to the editor was printed, I nearly died, I couldn't believe she said that considering mine was too! We almost didn't believe it. When I came home last night I checked and there the letters from each of us were with only two other letters between ours. It seemed incredible that two moms who didn't know each other, had sons who joined the Army for the same reason (9/11) and served in Iraq, wrote letters that appeared in the same newspaper on the same day quite unexpectedly found themselves sitting next to each other in a restaurant with our sons safely at the same table.*

The Hahn-Ward-Upton Family Newsletter (written especially for PFC Sean Ward) my dad wrote:

April 2003
GRANDMA HAHN-
Grandma will have a full knee replacement on May 6th – rehab for a week & before you know it she will be running the mile in under 4 minutes.

GRANDPA HAHN-

My golf game is really coming along. Recently played an 86, 88 and today 3/27 "82" not bad for an old guy like me (73 now). I'd join the senior tour but I'm too old.

JOHN HAHN-

He just pulled off a great deal. He sold Tri-City for a ton of money – John & Kevin invited all of us to Lake George in July – you were invited too – so check with your boss & tell him you need 2 wks off to be in Lake George in July. If he doesn't want to let you go tell him to call me – you are a very important member of the family & we need you home with us – who knows maybe he will see it our way – If you don't ask you don't get.

KEVIN HAHN & FAMILY-

Matt got a full scholarship from Penn State – you may or may not know the coach at Penn State – Joe Paterno sent Matt a personal letter (he's been the head coach for 100 years) thanking him picking Penn State.

Kevin Hahn (Kevy) is a champion wrestler – he recently won a gold medal and played great football – Matt's school St. Anthony's wants Kevin to play football for them – Kev is about 185 lbs and getting taller. Thank God all you guys and gals have some of my genes.

HANNAH AKA THE HAMMER –

She really can hit a softball – she has gotten really pretty – as matter of fact quite attractive – thank God she has grandma's genes.

CHRISTIAN –

Chris is probably the best 7 year old kid in the world – he is starting to play baseball & wants to be a quarterback. I had a catch with him one day and I was very impressed with his ability – thank God he has some of my genes.

JONATHON –

I saw Jonathon play baseball last year in the playoffs – I was glad I took the trip (I really love seeing all of you guys & gals play sports) – Jonathon really played great – hitting and fielding was super – we also caught a few basketball games – he is really getting good in basketball – he is getting so tall & very athletic – and a great kid.

JESSICA –

We were so lucky recently we had your mom & pop – Jess and the girls & Terry & Chris & Hannah at our house – my older brother & sister had some long talks with your mom & dad and were so impressed with them – It was really great to have my side of the family meet all my kids & grandchildren. Jess looks great – lost a lot of weight.

NICOLE –

Nicole played the flute every once in a while – she really plays great. She also runs around singing all the time – I think she ought to sing country western.

CAROLYN –

Carolyn ran around protecting all the insects & bugs in the whole neighborhood. She kept her eye on the alligator – she thought he or she was really neat – every once in a while the alligator swims by the house calling Carolyn, Carolyn, where are you............

KELLY –

Well she is so independent – probably the most independent kid in the world – the girls & Chris were playing football on the side of the house and I never saw any kid her age that could run as fast as Kelly.

VISIT TO NORTH CAROLINA –

Grandma & I drove to visit mom, pop & Kate – we first thought we would visit you at Ft. Stewart but you ran off on vacation to the Mid-East – I guess it was a cheap trip – anyway we love the new house and it was really great to visit Mary, Tom & Kate – I gave Kate my 1989 red Buick to Kate – its being shipped up today 3/27/03. She already gave it a name – Tonto – get it Red car – I guess I didn't tell you we bought a 2004 Grand Marquis Florida Edition with all the bells and whistles – great 4 door six passenger – Oh I forgot to tell you Grandma gets the new car and I get the second hand Lexus –

Well Sean I ran out of gas – I've never written a letter in my life more than 4 or 5 lines – I guess you mean a lot to me – We all pray every day for your safety – quick return home – We all think about you all the time.

We love you very much. Don't take any chances with any of those Iraqis.

Love, Grandpa Hahn

I found my email prayer voice one more time and shared it with Carol. Carol sent it to me in the prayer book she made for us:

4/18/2003
Let me see. I can find a prayer.
    How life changes, huh? We have never been
alone for Easter and here we are ready or not.
Maybe we will go find the beach for the day. We
will need to do something totally different to get
through this day..

Dear Jesus:
    You gave your life for us. We are grateful forev-
er that you came into our lives and blessed us with
the family we have. You helped us find strength and
integrity in our darkest hours. You helped us learn
to embrace the challenges and face them straight on
especially when we thought we couldn't take anoth-
er thing. We still have more to do, some of which
will not be so easy and some we will rejoice in.
    Please continue to hold our hands as we walk
through life with you. Your touch is essential to
feeding us what we need to get the best job done.
    Amen.

Lastly, a few weeks after the homecoming we received a note
and poem written by a wonderful family friend and published
poet, Fran Morgan:

Dear dear Mary, Tom, Sean and Katie,
    We are overjoyed for you all that Sean is home!
Thank God! All of our prayers have been answered!
Praise be to Jesus and His Blessed Mother, for He
Who is Mighty has done great things for the Ward
and Hahn families!
    I wrote this poem after watching Sean and
Mary on MSNBC-TV. You both looked so beauti-
ful, handsome and happy.
    You have all earned your crowns in Heaven for

what you all went through since Sean went to war.
  Frantastic love,
  Fran Morgan

THE JOYFUL DAY PFC SEAN WARD RETURNED FROM THE WAR IN IRAQ BY FRAN MORGAN

One hundred angels were gathered
They were praising the Lord,
For bringing home safe and sound
PFC Sean T. Ward

He fought for his country
Night and day in Iraq.
Earth Angels beseeched God
To please bring him back.
His safety, our focus, while he was away,
We wrote, and sent goodies, and continued to pray.
He'd seen all the carnage of 9-11-01
When twenty terrorists killed thousands, and
The war had begun.
A Volunteer Firefighter, he was moved to do right,
And for his brothers and country
He decided to fight.

Enlisting in the Army
He was sent into war.
And "grew up" very quickly
As they settled the score.

In the roasting hot desert,
In hundred ten degrees,
Carried rifle, flak jacket,
With never a breeze.

The primary lesson he learned in Iraq
Was to be alert always, and to cover his back.

He saw soldiers murdered
By enemy fire
And fought bravely on
Through fear, dust and mire.

He remembered his loved ones
With cards and cell phone
Always aware, that they felt so alone.

His return with 800 of great marching men
Was a feast for our eyes, and a grateful "AMEN"

One hundred Angels, his guardians
From the day of his birth,
Joined his Angels on earth's prayers
For all were worth.

And God, in His mercy
Brought home our dear boy
August 8, 2003, the best day of great joy!
Welcome home, Sean! We love you!

GLOSSARY

1Lt. – First Lieutenant is an officer pay grade between a second lieutenant and a captain. They wear one silver bar on their collar.

Abrams – The name of the U.S. Army tank currently in use.

AK47 – Named after a Russian weapons designer Anatoly Kulisnakov. It is a standard issue rifle for many of the world's Armies.

ARCOM – Army Commendation Medal - The Army Commendation Medal is awarded to any member of the Armed Forces of the United States other than General Officers who, while serving in any capacity with the Army after 6 December 1941, distinguished himself by heroism, meritorious achievement or meritorious service.

ARCOM with a V device – See above. "V" is for valor and is represented by a small metallic letter "V" attached to the ARCOM ribbon worn on the dress uniform.

Basic Rifle Marksmanship – A segment of basic training that familiarizes the recruit with the function and operation of the M-16 rifle.

Batt. – Battalion. A battalion is a group of soldiers ranging ranging from 400 to 1000.

BDU – Battle Dress Uniform. This is the camouflage uniform the soldiers typically wear on a daily basis.

BMP – Russian style armored personal carrier.

Boomy cap – a soft hat worn by soldiers with a wide brim.

Bradley – Bradley Fighting Vehicle. The Bradley uses tracks like a bulldozer and carries six to eight infantrymen into battle.

CentCom – Central Command. Central Command is located in Tampa,Florida. The war was managed from Central Command.

Chinook – is a twin rotor helicopter that carries approximately 20 to 30 Infantrymen into combat.

CIB – Combat Infantryman Badge. The blue and silver badge worn by Infantrymen only after they have taken fire from an enemy in combat. The badge is a Kentucky longrifle inside a wreath.

Click – One kilometer

CO – Commanding officer

Concertina wire – Coils of barbed wire with razor blades on it.

DCU top – Desert camouflage uniform jacket

DS – Drill Sergeant - the person who trains new recruits at basic training.

Drive on – A motivational statement intended to encourage the soldier to continue with the mission.

EOD – Explosive ordinance detail – they dispose of unexploded bombs.

EIB – Expert Infantryman Badge. Awarded to an infantryman after qualifying on a rigorous course of infantry skills.

Elcan M145 – A telescopic sight for machine guns.

Full Battle Rattle – An infantryman is said to be in full battle rattle when he is wearing all his gear including flak jacket, helmet, knee pads, ammunition pouches, etc. because it tends to rattle when he walks.

Garrison – A base where troops are stationed.

Green to Gold – This is when an enlisted soldier becomes an officer.

Guidon – The long wood pole that carries the small unit flag for a platoon or company of men.

Haji – This is the name an Iraqi calls someone who completes the Muslim pilgrimage required of them. The pilgrimage is called the Haj.

Hasty – Similar to a shallow grave dug to protect the soldier from enemy fire.

Infantry (Infantrymen) – Soldiers who fight primarily on foot, using personal weapons. The term infantrymen is reserved for the most basic of infantry troops, the riflemen. Not all soldiers are infantrymen.

Latrine – The soldiers call the toilet a latrine.

Live HE rounds – HE means High Explosive and live means the rounds are not duds; they are capable of exploding.

M16A4 – The rifle currently used by the military.

M249SAW – A machine gun used by the military. SAW is a squad automatic weapon.

MOS – Military Occupational Specialty. A code number is assigned to the Occupation. Infantry is an 11b (pronounced eleven bravo).

MOUT Training – Urban warfare training for house-to-house fighting. Ex. Soldiers learn to kick down doors.

MRE – Meals ready to eat. These are the meals the soldiers eat when they are in the field.

Paladins – A self propelled Howitzer or canon.

PX – Post Exchange. It is similar to a general store located on Army bases.

RPG7 – Rocket Propelled Grenade. It is a long tube used as a grenade launcher.

ROE – Rules of engagement – these are written rules that determine when a soldier may shoot at the enemy.

Rucksack – A small knapsack a soldier uses.

SKS – A Russian rifle.

SGT – Abbreviation for sergeant.

SSG – Staff Seargant. A non-commissioned officer.

Turning Blue Ceremony – The color of infantry is blue. Turning Blue is an impressive ceremony specifically assigned for Infantry. One of his family members or other loved ones will be given the opportunity to attach the blue Infantry cord to his Class a uniform.

Acknowledgements

This book was possible through the efforts of many people especially my son, Sean. He shared his heart and soul, his successes and challenges in his letters and graciously agreed to publish them.

I've been extremely fortunate to have good people in my life that believed in this project from the beginning and here they are:

Tom, my husband; my children, Kate and Sean, for reading the early drafts and giving me their honest feedback; my parents, John and Carol Hahn, for listening to me talk of almost nothing else these past few months and having the confidence to invest in my self-publishing dream, and most importantly for sharing in my worries while Sean was at war and being there the day he came home; to Carol Hayter Bomba and Pat Nicholas for reading the first unedited draft and finding the story rather than the errors, they are the ones who encouraged me to continue writing; to Tracey Koepke for taking the time to read, edit and share her thoughts with me on how I can improve the book; to Deb Lapolice for taking control of my grammar and having the patience to teach me how to improve my style without losing my voice; to Margaret Cooney for seeing the big picture and helping me to organize my thoughts; to Lacey Chylack for agreeing to work with me and teaching me the finer details of publishing and most importantly for designing a dignified, warm cover and interior for which I will forever be grateful; and finally to our family and friends who were there for us through our darkest and brightest moments during Operation Iraqi Freedom.

ABOUT THE AUTHOR

Mary Ward, MS, MPA, formerly of Cornwall, NY currently lives in Durham, NC with her husband Tom. *Letters Home* is her first book.